# "WHAT EVERY HUSBAND & WIFE SHOULD KNOW BEFORE IT'S TOO LATE"

By

ALVIN B. BARANOV, JD

&

ESTHER SIRKIN, DD

Published By:

## Legal Publications, Inc.

6931 Van Nuys Boulevard, Van Nuys, California 91405

Library of Congress Catalog Card Number: 77-93768
ISBN 0-89031-027-X Trade
ISBN 0-89031-027-9 Soft Cover
Printed in the United States of America


Typesetting by
Lucas Graphics
Canoga Park, California

Printing by
Delta Lithograph
Van Nuys, California

# TABLE OF CONTENTS

# INTRODUCTION

Part I of this book concerns the importance about communication between husband and wife concerning their marital assets and information a wife should have in the event of her husband's dying. We suggest that every husband and wife study and read this book together. We want every husband to know that we respect his feelings because this book, in reality, applies as much to him as to his wife.

Avoiding the subject of death is in keeping with the fears of many. However, it is a fact that must eventually be faced and we have approached this subject in a realistic manner.

The loss of a spouse is a traumatic experience. The loss may be sudden, resulting in extreme shock, emotional distress, nervous breakdown, frustration, and a sense of futility.

The loss may be the result of a short or unexpected illness or accident or the loss may be anticipated. The loss may even be a relief to the spouse, the family, and even possibly to the deceased. Nevertheless, the occurrence of death is painful to the ones who are left behind.

The United States Census Bureau and many insurance companies employ experts called actuaries who prepare statistics recording the extent, among other things, to which women outlive men. Recent studies have established that wives outlive husbands at a ratio of three to two. Because of this possibility we are focusing our attention on the necessity and importance for preparation for the time when a wife might be left alone and what she should be prepared to do in that event.

This book is intended to make both husband and wife aware of the possible legal and emotional results that could occur. Its main purpose is to make husband and wife realize the importance and necessity of the information and knowledge that each must have concerning their economic affairs. This information is extremely necessary to enable each spouse to handle not only the responsibilities that will arise in the administration of an estate, but also to help cope with any emotional crisis that may arise.

When a husband dies, the primary question that arises in the minds of most surviving wives is *"WHAT DO I DO NOW?"* This question applies not only to the widow's feeling of aloneness, fear and uncertainty, but also to her economic future and social status.

The question *"WHAT DO I DO NOW?"* requires answers, the preparation for which should begin long before the husband dies.

It is the wise husband who discusses with his wife the details of his business, the extent of their holdings, and their marital finances. Every couple should frankly and openly discuss their debts and obligations, jointly held assets, as well as their separate property, should there be any. It is never too early to delve into these matters—but it could be too late.

Every husband should ask himself questions such as the following:

1. To what extent has he discussed his business with his wife.
2. To what extent is his wife involved in the over-all management of the financial aspects of their marriage.
3. Does his wife know how to handle money?
4. Is she capable of making sensible decisions concerning investments and property?
5. Would she have the foresight to seek competent advise?
6. Is she really interested in these matters?

If a wife has had no experience in the management of money or business training, she will encounter many problems in handling her financial future when she is alone.

Far too many wives are kept in the dark by their husbands in the mistaken belief that they are protecting them and making life easier for them. *NOTHING IS FURTHER FROM THE TRUTH!* Unless a wife has complete knowledge of all of the details of her husband's business, his personal data, his separate property, if any, and their jointly owned assets, she could possibly lose much of what her husband intended her to have upon his death. This has occurred too many times to be ignored. The tremendous effort of attempting to learn these facts at this critical time could be a confusing and depressing experience.

Where there has been little exchange of information between husband and wife, the wife will not be adequately prepared to assume new or perhaps overwhelming responsibilities should her husband die. For instance, a wife who has been over-protected by her husband may never have paid rent, utilities, bills, etc., she may not even know how to write a check correctly or how to keep accurate records. To assemble all the information that is required in the administration of an estate takes a great deal of time, ingenuity, imagination, and clear thinking.

When a husband shares all the information he alone possesses with his wife he will eliminate the necessity for her exerting time and effort, or experiencing emotional stress. Even money may be saved. This knowledge will help ease the wife's transition from the married state to sudden singleness.

Newly bereaved wives are generally so emotionally distraught that unless they have been given complete information by their husbands they will find it extremely difficult to bring themselves to the task of assembling all of the information required for probate proceedings, administration of the estate, and the filing of assorted claims for Social Security, insurance, and pensions benefits.

To many wives, the thought never occurs that the loss of their husbands could create untold personal, practical, social, and emotional problems. If any thought of loss of her husband is suggested to a wife, many will merely shrug it off and answer, "It can't happen to me." BUT IT DOES! And then the question is asked in all despair, *"WHAT DO I DO NOW?"*

With these thoughts in mind, we will discuss in depth the preparation that should be undertaken to help a surviving wife to take over and handle the legal, practical and emotional problems of widowhood.

Part II of this book describes the emotional, psychological and social aspects of widowhood. These will be examined by Esther Sirkin, D.D. Director of the Institute for The Science of Living, Van Nuys, Calif.

# CHAPTER 1

## *Part One*

# PREPARING A WIFE FOR INDEPENDENCE

A great many wives are ill prepared to face the consequences of being on their own. Few women realize the opportunity to learn or develop a capacity for economic independence while married. Unless a husband leaves a large estate which produces an income sufficient to take care of all the needs of a wife and family, most wives will find their lifestyle necessarily reduced.

More and more couples are realizing the necessity of preparing a wife to earn her own living. Many wives will seek employment long before their husbands die and in doing so, will gain experience and perhaps new interests. Because of the federal government's equal opportunity laws, more and more opportunities in formerly male-dominated employment areas are now opening up to women. In most instances, women are proving successful at performing the same jobs as men.

So, we suggest that the best time for wives to begin preparation is while they are young. In those instances where the wife has never worked for any extended time or is not prepared in any given field, her first determination must be that of deciding what she would like to do. After selecting a job category or several job categories, the United States Department of Labor, Women's Bureau, can provide information of programs and schools designed especially for women. In practically every city the Chamber of Commerce or Municipal Bureau have lists of schools where various courses are available.

Some thought should be given by a working wife to her future employment if her husband should pass away. She should decide whether she would be satisfied doing what she is presently doing or if she can improve her skills by further study. We suggest that you do what is best for you and set out to achieve a goal.

# CHAPTER 2

# PREPARATION FOR WIDOWHOOD

Since statistics have established that there are far more widows than widowers, it behooves every married couple to give considerable thought now to what information every wife should have concerning her husband's personal data and their marital affairs should she become a widow.

It is never to a husband's advantage to conceal vital information that his wife could someday need. If a husband feels that his wife is important to him, he should have no hesitancy in furnishing her with all the information pertaining to him personally and all details of their marital assets.

When a husband intentionally withholds details of his business and the facts about their marital economics he is being dishonest. If anything should happen to him the wife will be at a complete loss. Failing to share this knowledge with his wife is actually being disloyal to her.

When a wife shows interest in her husband's business, his brainstorming, and in the management of their marital properties, he will naturally be willing to provide her with complete information.

Many husbands are reluctant to discuss these matters with their wives because such a discussion may be embarrassing to them, or they may be frightened to discuss death, or they may simply refuse to face reality. Perhaps some husbands do not want their wives to know certain facts. As a result of being kept in the dark, a great many wives are left pitifully ignorant of matters that will concern them most when they are at the bottom emotionally. We must again emphasize that every wife should know everything about her husband's business, his personal data, his separate property, if any, and their jointly owned assets. Wives should have absolutely no reluctance nor fear to ask their husbands to talk with them about these matters—before it is too late. And husbands should have no reluctance to share their knowledge with their wives.

If a husband is reticent about furnishing the information on pages 8 to 27, or refuses to do so, the wife should be, at first, pleasantly persuasive in seeking the needed answers.

Since it is universally known that most husbands want to provide security for their wives and families, a wife should have no hesitancy in saying to her husband, "I know you care for me and our family and want to provide for us. By sharing details and information about your business, our marriage assets, and our mutally owned property, you will make things so much easier for me should you pass away before I do. Then I will have all of the information that I need to handle problems that may arise. It will make the administration of your estate much simpler. It could also help make it easier for me to cope with my emotions.''

With this approach, your husband will be more than likely to co-operate. No healthy man enjoys the thought of dying or even talking about it. If your husband treats your request lightly or passes it off entirely, we suggest that you impress upon him that without your having this necessary information you will be compelled, while under intense emotional strain, to undertake a task completely foreign to you. Tell him you may have to make an investigation and search to gather the facts that he can so easily provide. It is far better for you to resist some discomfiture and perhaps some unpleasantness at this time than to face the tremendous task of assembling all the information you will need at a time when you can least afford to do so emotionally. Only your husband can give you peace of mind by furnishing you with this information.

All this information is of utmost importance, not only in the preparation of probate documents, estate and inheritance tax returns, but also in the filing of claims for Social Security benefits, benefits from federal, state and municipal governments, filing proof of claims for insurance, pension, retirement and profit sharing plans.

## CHAPTER 3

# TOPICS TO BE DISCUSSED

To assist you and your spouse to understand what is essential, we have prepared a list of subjects dividing them into several categories. Some of the subjects may appear to be irrelevant, but may be required by a probate court, a federal or state taxing agency, or in a claim for benefits.

We suggest you do not attempt to go over all of the items on the following pages at one time. Discuss a few of them at a time in detail. Do not rely on memory. All the facts should be written in duplicate and kept in separate safe places. Be sure to note the name and location of banks, savings and loan associations, bond and savings account numbers, the location of safe deposit boxes and keys. Note where all other important papers and securities are kept. Make a note of all identifying numbers on all documents.

It is recommended wherever possible both spouses record individual answers.

# PERSONAL AND MARITAL DATA

1. Full name of husband, date and place of birth, and social security number.

2. Wife's maiden name, date and place of birth, and social security number.

3. Date and place of marriage.

4. Names, birthdates, addresses and social security number of all children of this marriage.

5. Names, addresses, place of birth of husband's parents and of wife's parents, maiden names of husband and wife's mothers.

6. Names, birthdates, addresses of husband and wife's brothers, sisters and their children.

7. Husband's education: highest school grade completed. Name of college, date of graduation and degree, if any.

8. Wife's education: highest school grade completed. Name of college, date of graduation and degree, if any.

9. Husband and wife's military service.
   a.  Date and place of induction into service:
   b.  Branch of service:
   c.  Serial number:

   d.  Date and place of discharge:
   e.  Rank at time of discharge:
   f.  Foreign service. Location and dates.
   g.  Military honors:

10.  If either was retired from military service:
   a.  Date and place of retirement and rank.
   b.  Does either receive a pension? Amount?
   c.  Reason for retirement.

11.  If either was discharged from military service because of service-connected disability state:
   a.  Nature of disability.
   b.  Date and rank at time of discharge.
   c.  Does either receive a pension? Amount?

12.  If either was hospitalized at any Veteran's Administration Hospital state:
   a.  Location of hospital.
   b.  Reason for hospitalization, and date.
   c.  Date of discharge from hospital.

13.  If either was discharged from military service because of a non-military connected disability, state:
   a.  State disability.
   b.  Rank at date of discharge.
   c.  Does either receive a pension? Amount?

14.  If either is receiving any Veteran's pension or benefits, state reason and amount received.

## PREVIOUS MARRIAGE

15. If husband was previously married, state:
    a. Previous wife's maiden name, age, birthdate, place of birth, present name and address, if known.
    b. State date and place of marriage.

16. State how previous marriage was terminated.
    a. If by death, state cause, date and place.
        (1). If former wife's estate was probated, state: when, location of court, details of distribution of estate assets.
    b. If by dissolution or divorce state:
        (1). Name and address of court.
        (2). Grounds.
        (3). Where, date and who received the divorce ordissolution decree. Names and address of attorneys.

17. If there was a marital or property settlement agreement and/or agreement for alimony and/or child support, who has copy?

18. Where are the divorce or dissolution files.

19. State names, birthdates, and place of birth of children of previous marriage. State recent addresses.

20. If alimony and/or child support was ordered by court or agreed upon, state:

    a.  If husband is presently making payments state amount, to whom, and addresses of payees.

21. State names, birthdates, addresses of any grandchildren of previous marriage and names and addresses of their parents.

## WILL

22. Has husband or wife prepared a will?
    a.  Where is it kept? It is suggested that the original and copies of the will be kept in places that are easily accessible.

23. Has either prepared a codicil to the will?
    a.  Where is it kept?

24. If there are any former wills, have they been destroyed?

25. Witnesses to the will:
    a.  State name, address and telephone number of each witness to latest will and/or codicil.

26. Has either provided in a will for any minor child by previous marriage?
    a.  State provisions.
    b.  Names, addresses and date of birth of each child provided for. It should be noted that most states require that all children should be

mentioned in a will whether or not any bequest is made to them.

27. Has either provided in a will for any adult child of a previous marriage? In most states they must be mentioned in a will whether or not any bequest is made to them.
   a. State provisions.
   b. Names, ages, addresses and date of birth of each adult child.

28. Has either provided in a will for any grandchild of a previous marriage?
   a. State provisions.
   b. Names, addresses and dates of birth of each grandchild.

29. How have children of present marriage been provided for. In most states they must be mentioned whether or not any bequest is made to them.
   a. State provisions.
   b. Names, addresses and dates of birth of each child.

30. Have either provided for any other relatives or friends in the will?
   a. State names, addresses and telephone numbers.

31. Does either have any objections to any such provisions in the wills. State objections.

32. Do both have a copy of present will?

33. State names, addresses and telephone numbers of persons nominated in each will to act as personal representative.

34. State names, addresses, and telephone numbers of attorney(s).

35. Does will provide for a marital deduction? If not, an attorney should be consulted for advice concerning the advantages of such a provision in the will. See section "Diminishing Tax Consequence Of An Estate" page 33.

36. Have wills been updated and/or changed to meet present conditions.

## ASSETS

37. Do spouses have a safe deposit box?
   a. Location of box and keys. Prepare a list of contents in safe deposit box for each spouse to keep.

38. Who has access to the safe deposit box? It is suggested that if the box is in the husband's name alone, the signature card be changed to permit the wife to enter the box. It is also suggested that if husband and wife are the sole shareholders and officers of a corporation, the safe deposit box should be registered in the name of the corporation with both husband and wife authorized to enter the box so that upon the death of either spouse,

the survivor may have immediate access to the safe deposit box.

39. List major items of personal property such as antiques, furniture, piano, television set, stereo, and (a) state cost of each (b) date of acquisition (c) location.

40. List make, model, year, and license number of all automobiles, motorcycles, trucks, vans, motor homes, etc. (a) state how title to each is held (b) cost of each (c) date of acquisition of each.

41. List all credit cards and credit accounts. State in whose name the charge or credit account is carried.

42. List location of each bank, savings and loan association and the identifying account numbers of each.
   a. State in whose name each account is held. It is recommended that all accounts be held in joint names so as to permit easy withdrawal by the survivor. (See Joint Tenancy Page 30.)

## PERSONAL DATA

43. State names, addresses and telephone numbers of husband and wife's doctor or doctors.

44. State names, addresses and telephone numbers of husband and wife's financial advisors and attorneys.

45. If either is a party to any pending litigation, state the following:
   a. Name of parties.
   b. Name of court and address, case number.
   c. Names, addresses and telephone numbers of attorneys for both sides.
   d. Name and address of adverse party.
   e. Nature of lawsuit.
   f. Location of pertinent files and particulars pertaining to the case.
   g. Status of the case.
   h. Names, addresses and telephone numbers of all witnesses and a summary of their anticipated testimony.

46. If either have any unsatisfied judgments (a judgement is the decision in a legal action) against them, list the following:
   a. Name of parties.
   b. Name of court and address, case number.
   c. Names and addresses of all attorneys.
   d. Names, addresses and telephone numbers of parties holding the judgments.
   e. Amount of judgment remaining unsatisfied.
   f. Location of pertinent files and papers pertaining to the case.

47. If either have any unpaid judgments in their favor, list the following:
   a. Name of parties.
   b. Name and address of courts, case numbers.

   c. Names, addresses and telephone numbers of husband's attorneys and defendants attorneys.

   d. Nature of case.

   e. Defendants' names, addresses and telephone numbers.

   f. What is the amount of the judgment and present unpaid balance. Date of last payment and amount.

   g. Location of pertinent files pertaining to the lawsuit.

48. If there are any disputes where litigation may be instituted against husband, wife or both, describe:

   a. Nature of the possible lawsuit.

   b. Names of parties involved.

   c. What is the present status of the dispute.

   d. Names, addresses and telephone numbers of all persons who may be involved, who have knowledge of the facts or may be called as a witness.

49. If an attorney has been consulted concerning the dispute, state name, address and telephone number of attorney. This is a very important subject which must be discussed in detail and all of the above information noted.

# PERSONAL DEBTS AND OBLIGATIONS

50. Names, addresses and telephone numbers of all creditors.

    a. Nature of debts or obligations.

    b. Amounts due to each.

    c. Date of last payment.

51. Debts and/or obligations due to husband and/or wife:

    a. Names, addresses and telephone number of each debtor.

    b. Nature of debt due, when due, amount and date of last payment.

# SECURITIES

Securities means any type of stocks, bonds, mortgages, trust deeds or other evidences of debts.

52. List type, name of security, identification number, amount of security, cost of acquisition, date of acquisition, estimated present value and how title is held.

Interest on bonds and some types of securities is paid by means of coupons attached to the bond or security which must be clipped from them for payment. These coupons can be redeemed for their face value by anyone presenting them to a bank as they are negotiable. Be careful not to lose them.

# REAL ESTATE

53. List all real estate owned by either husband or

wife as separate property:
  a. Legal description and address.
  b. Describe property (such as apartment house, dwelling, commercial property, etc.)
  c. Date of acquisition, acquisition cost and present estimated value.
  d. If income property, state annual income.

54. List all real property owned by husband and wife as community property or joint tenancy property.
  a. Legal description and address.
  b. Describe property (such as apartment house, dwelling, commercial property, etc.)
  c. Date of acquisition, acquisition cost and present estimated value.
  d. If income property, state annual income.

If you reside in a community property state, such as Arizona, California, Idaho, New Mexico, Nevada, Louisiana, Texas, or Washington, it is suggested that you consult an attorney pertaining to the community property rights of husband and wife.

55. List all real property owned by husband, wife, and/or husband and wife as tenants in common with each other or with others.
  a. Name all other such persons and describe their interest in the property.
  b. Legal description and address.
  c. Describe property (such as apartment house, dwelling, commercial property, etc.)

    d.  Date of acquisition, acquisition cost and present estimated value.

    e.  If income property, state annual income.

If husband and wife reside in a state other than a community property state, it is recommended that an attorney be consulted concerning the rights of husband and wife pertaining to jointly owned property.

# HOME

    56. If you own a home or are in the process of purchasing a home state:

    a.  How title is held.

    b.  Address and legal description.

    c.  Date of acquisition and acquisition costs.

    d.  Present value.

    57. If there is a mortgage or other encumbrance upon the property state:

    a.  Name and address of holder of the encumbrance.

    b.  Amount of monthly payments, present balance and date of month payable.

    c.  Maturity date of the encumbrance.

    58. List names and addresses of insurance agents or insurance companies. Describe insurance carried, amount of coverage, annual premiums and policy numbers.

## LIFE INSURANCE

59. List the following applicable to husband or wife:
   a. Name of insurance agency, insurance company, face amount of each life insurance policy, coverage of each policy, number of each policy, name of beneficiaries, yearly premium of each policy.

60. If there are paid-up policies, list:
   a. Name of company.
   b. Policy number.
   c. Face amount of policy.
   d. Cash surrender amount of policy.
   e. Beneficiary.

61. If there are loans against any policies, list the following:
   a. Name of company, policy and number.
   b. The face amount of the policy.
   c. Amount and date of loan.
   d. If there is a due date for payment, state date.

62. If there is a debt, mortgage redemption or credit life insurance policy (a policy that will pay off obligations upon death), state:
   a. Name of company.
   b. Policy number and annual premium.
   c. Total coverage.

63. If husband or wife carries accident, health or major medical insurance, list:

    a.  Name of agent and company.
    b.  Number of policy, annual premium.
    c.  Coverage, including death benefits.

64. Where are all insurance policies kept?

65. Other types of insurance: If you are covered with a public liability policy, list name of company, policy number, annual premium and coverage.

## SPECIAL INSURANCE AND PENSION BENEFITS

66. If husband or wife is an employee of a federal, state or municipal government and is covered by an insurance policy state:
    a.  Name and address of governmental agency.
    b.  Type of employment.
    c.  Where employed and what department.
    d.  Length of time employed.
    e.  Describe coverage and benefits.

67. If either has an annuity or special retirement plan, state:
    a.  Name and address of governmental agency.
    b.  Coverage and amount.
    c.  Amount contributed.
       tate:
    a.  Name, address and present balance of the accounts.

69. If either owes any money to a credit union, list name and address of credit union, amount due, how payable and when due.

70. Does membership in credit union provide any death benefits. Describe.

71. If either is receiving a pension, state name and address of payor and amount.

72. If either is entitled to any retirement benefits from any federal, state, or municipal government, state name and address of agency and describe retirement benefits and when due.

73. Do the federal, state, or municipal government retirement benefits provide for continued payment to wife or children after husband's death?

74. If either is retired and is receiving a pension from any federal, state, or municipal government, is he or she also covered for health and medical benefits. State name of agency, address and coverage.

75. Does the above coverage apply to wife and children after husband's death?

76. If either belongs to any fraternal organizations, list names and addresses of each.

77. Is either covered for any health, accident, or death benefits in any of the above named organizations? List organizations, addresses and describe benefits.

78. Does either desire his or her fraternal organization to participate in funeral service? Name organization, address and whom to contact.

## PRIVATE BUSINESS PENSION RETIREMENT OR PROFIT SHARING PLANS

79. If husband or wife is entitled to receive a pension or to participate in a profit sharing plan from private industry, state name and address of company, and describe pension or profit sharing plan.

80. If either is presently receiving a pension or participating in a profit sharing plan, list name and address of company, type of plan, date and amount being paid.

81. Will payment be continued to be paid to wife and/or children after husband's death?

82. If either is a director or officer of any corporation state the official position, name and address of corporation.

83. If either is a director or officer of a corporation, is either covered by any type of insurance or entitled to health, accident, major medical or death benefits? List name of company and describe benefits.

## BUSINESS

84. If husband or wife owns any patents or copyrights list:
   a.   Describe patent or copyright.
   b.   Patent or copyright number.
   c.   Date of patent or copyright.
   d.   Name, address of patent copyright attorney.

85. If either receives any royalties on patents or copyrights, list: Name and address of company, amounts or percentages paid.

86. Where are royalty contracts kept?

87. List all businesses and addresses in which husband or wife has an interest, and the extent of the interest.

88. List all occupational licenses and permits issued to husband or wife (federal, state or municipal.)

89. If husband or wife is in the real estate development business, describe type of development, location, names and addresses or associates, name of lending agencies, if any, methods and terms of repayment of loans, location or main office.

90. State location and name of person in possession of all business records, accounts and ledgers.

91. Names, addresses and telephone numbers of business accountants.

92. If husband or wife is a member of a partnership, list:
   a. Name and address of partnership and type of business.
   b. What is husband or wife's share of the partnership.
   c. Names, addresses and telephone numbers of each partner and their respective interest in the partnership.

93. Where is partnership agreement kept?

94. Does partnership agreement provide for sale of partner's interest to surviving partner/partners in the event of death.
   a. Are partner's interests covered by life insurance.
   b. Does the agreement provide that the surviving spouse of a deceased partner shall become a member of the partnership.
   c. Does the agreement provide for continued existence after the death of a partner.

95. What is partnership's present value?

96. Who is the general manager of the partnership?

97. What is the authority and duty of each partner?

98. What is the husband or wife's authority and duties in the partnership?

99. List the assets and liabilities of the partnership?
   a. Where is the last financial report of the partnership?

100. Where are and who has charge of the partnership books and records?
   a. What is the name, address and telephone number of partnership accountant.

101. Does partnership have any judgments in its favor? Describe in detail. List balances due.

102. Does the partnership have any judgments against it? Describe in detail. List balances due.

103. List location, description, value of all the partnership real estate and how title is held.

104. Describe partnership's personal property, such as office equipment and motor vehicles with identifying license plate numbers. Where is the property located and what is its value?

105. If the partnership owes husband or wife money for cash advanced to the partnership, salary or for profits due, list amounts, when and how to be paid and at what rate of interest.

In many cases a wife should furnish information to her husband which she alone possesses. This applies to situations where a wife owns separate property or has accumulated and banked funds earned by either or both of them without disclosing the name or location of the depository. There are many cases where a wife has failed to disclose a name and location of a depository of funds. By not disclosing this fact to her husband, to a trusted relative or family friend, the property eventually was lost to the state because it was never claimed.

We have attempted to list all the information that should be exchanged between husband and wife. If we have omitted any subjects, we suggest you include them in the written notations that you will be making.

It is further recommended that husband and wife review all of the above periodically and make necessary changes.

# CHAPTER 4

# PROPERTY

## SEPARATE PROPERTY

Separate property has been defined as all property owned by either spouse before marriage and all property acquired by either spouse after marriage by gift, bequest, devise or descent. The status of separate property is determined as of the time when the property was acquired. The owner of separate property has the absolute power of disposition of it without regard to any other person. Separate property includes pensions and any monetary award for personal injuries made to a spouse.

## COMMUNITY PROPERTY

The community property states are Arizona, California, Idaho, Louisiana, Nevada, New Mexico, Texas, and Washington. Community property is defined as all compensation earned by husband or wife after marriage and all property acquired with those earnings, with each owning an undivided one-half of such property regardless of which spouse earned it.

Property owned before marriage or received by either

spouse through gift, descent or devise is not community property but the separate property of the spouse receiving it. This means that the recipient is the owner of 100% of such property to the exclusion of the other spouse.

In the community property states, a spouse can only will away his or her one-half share of the community property and no more, the other half being owned absolutely by the surviving spouse. Occasionally, some property may be held in the name of one spouse alone. If that property was acquired with community funds, it is community property. In most states neither spouse can transfer community property without the written consent of the other.

## JOINT TENANCY

Many states recognize the concept of joint tenancy ownership of property acquired by two or more persons. Joint tenancy has been defined as "a joint interest in property owned by two or more persons in equal shares by a title created by a single will or transfer." The most common example of joint tenancy property is one in which husband and wife purchase a home and take title to the property as "John Doe and Mary Doe, husband and wife as joint tenants."

Joint tenancy differs from community property in that either joint tenant can terminate the joint tenancy character of the property by simply transfering his or her share to another person. The transfer of community property, on the other hand, requires the consent and signature of both husband and wife. The distinguishing feature of joint tenancy is the right of survivorship. This means that upon death of either joint tenant, the joint tenancy property belongs entirely to the surviving joint tenant to the exclusion of heirs of the deceased. Another distinguishing feature is that a joint tenant cannot bequeath his or her interest in joint tenancy property by will since upon death, the property automatically belongs to the surviving joint tenant. Joint tenancy property is not subject to probate proceedings.

Before taking title to real property, it would be advisable to consult an attorney to determine the most advantagious manner in which to take title.

Since the laws pertaining to separate property, community property and joint tenancy property vary from state to state, it is recommended that an attorney be consulted in your state to determine your rights with regard to separate, community, or joint tenancy property.

**CHAPTER 5**

# DIMINISHING THE TAX CONSEQUENCES OF AN ESTATE

While this book is not a work on taxation, this chapter is designed to bring to the attention of both husband and wife the use of legal devices which can reduce and in some instances eliminate estate and inheritance taxes. These are taxes levied by both the federal government and the various states upon the transfer of property upon death either by will (probate) or by intestate proceedings. Because the manner and method of levying state inheritance taxes and the rate of inheritance taxes vary from state to state, it is not practical to discuss them in detail here.

Regardless of the value of an estate we suggest that an expert in estate planning be consulted. The savings in estate and inheritance taxes could very well far exceed the expense incurred.

On January 1, 1977, the new Federal Estate and Gift Tax Reform Act of 1976 became effective. Among the most drastic and far reaching changes was the increase in the federal exemption on estate taxes and increase in amount of the marital deduction. Because of these changes many estates will not be required to pay federal estate taxes. However, the new federal law does not affect the rates of the various state inheritance taxes. The federal estate tax is a tax levied by the federal government upon estates that exceed the new estate tax exemption.

The tax must be paid nine months after the death of a spouse unless an extension of time has been granted. Failure to file the federal estate tax return form 706 and to pay the estate tax could result in interest and penalties being levied.

In arriving at the net amount of the taxable estate, specific deductions are permitted to be subtracted from the total or gross estate. The federal estate tax return 706, in cases where it is required, must be prepared and must include all the assets owned in which the decedent held an interest, such as, partnerships, insurance policies, separate real and personal property, real and personal property owned in conjunction with some other person, such as community property or joint tenancy property.

While death taxes result in erosion of an estate, the amount of depletion can be legally controlled by the use of a number of recognized legal devices.

Among the legal devices are gifts from one spouse to the other (not taxable if not made in contemplation of death); gifts to charities; ownership of life insurance policies which will be discussed later; marital deductions; revocable and irrevocable living trusts and testamentary trusts.

Because of the many ramifications of the new Federal Estate and Gift Tax Reform Act, it is recommended that a tax attorney or bank trust officer be consulted with respect to the use of any tax saving devices.

## MARITAL DEDUCTIONS

The new tax regulations have increased the maximum estate tax marital deductions for property passing from a decedent to a surviving spouse to the greater of 50 percent of the estate or $250,000. Therefore, unless the adjusted gross estate amounts to $500,000 or more, the federal estate tax consequences will be minimal or, at best, nonexistent. In the event the taxable estate exceeds the exemption, the use of the marital deduction would be practical.

It should be noted that in the community property states, only one-half of the community property is required to be included in the decedent's gross estate. In the case of a decedent's separate property, a similar split is accomplished indirectly by means of the marital deduction. The practical effect therefore of the marital deduction along with the income-splitting provisions of the federal income tax law is to establish for federal estate tax purposes the concept that property belonging to one spouse belongs equally to the other. However this concept does not change the property rights of the individuals.

## TRUSTS

A trust has been defined as a written agreement in which a person, for example, the husband, (sometimes called a trustor, donor, grantor, or settlor) transfers all or a portion of his property to a third person or institution such as a bank or trust company with directions to carry out specific purposes. If the trust purposes are carried out during the life of the trustor, it is called a living trust. The trust agreement must name the trustee, the beneficiary of the trust, describe the use of the trust income, the management of trust assets, and the disposition of the trust property upon death. The trustor can specify any conditions he wishes which must be followed to the letter by the trustee. In some instances, a trust can be created so that the income and all or a portion of the estate can continue through two or three generations. If the trust is created by a will, it is called a testamentary trust.

There are two types of living trusts. The revocable and the irrevocable living trust. By using either the revocable or the irrevocable living trust, probate may be avoided, and under some circumstances, the necessity of filing federal estate tax return form 706, and state inheritance tax return can be avoided.

The revocable living trust is one over which the trustor has ultimate control. That is, he may, during his lifetime revoke the trust, retake the possession and control of the property or trust assets. The revocable trust generally does not result in any estate tax savings. The irrevocable living trust is one that upon its execution by the trustor, cannot be revoked or terminated. It is the irrevocable living trust that results in both federal and estate tax savings under new law.

While many wives may resist the creation of a living trust by the husband and the placing of property in the hands of a trustee, there is an advantage for the wife's benefit. If the wife is inexperienced in business matters and in the management of real estate, incapable of handling large sums of money, does not understand bookkeeping or simply is not interested in assuming responsibility of the administering her husband's estate, the execution of a revocable or irrevocable trust should be seriously considered. Once again, we suggest, that a tax attorney, a bank's trust officer or an estate planning counselor be consulted.

## CHAPTER 6

# PREPARATION FOR THE FUTURE

## WILLS

In general terms, a will has been defined as a written document directing the disposition of a decedent's property, dated and signed by the maker in the presence of witnesses. But a will is much more than just a document! A will can be the most controlling factor in a widow's future. Its importance is manifested by the fact that it is the final direction by a husband for the disposition and distribution of his estate.

Most every husband has the desire to leave his estate with as little confustion and few problems as possible. This can be accomplished by a husband making a will with specific directions concerning the distribution of property which he is entitled to bequeath. Before a will is prepared an inventory of assets should be made and then time taken by husband and wife to discuss their distribution. Of course, consideration should be given to bequests to children. In some states, failure to mention or provide in some manner for children will result in the children inheriting as though there were no will, that is, as in an intestate proceeding.

Some husbands are fearful or reluctant to leave all income producing property or large sums outright to their wives for the reason that their wives may lack business experience, ability to make decisions or the power to resist unscrupulous persons. To insure that his estate will not be dissipated and to provide safeguards for his wife a husband should consider making appropriate provisions in his will. There are many alternatives and in arriving at a decision a husband should consider the following:

1. Should all of the estate be distributed to his wife at one time?
2. Should all of the cash in the estate be distributed to her in a lump sum?
3. Should he set up a trust for her with income to be paid in specified amounts at specific times for life and upon her death the remainder to be distributed to children or others?
4. Should he provide that the wife shall be given a life estate and upon her death the remainder to be given to children or others?

Since the laws of trusts and life estates vary from state to state, the advice and guidance of a competent attorney or trust officer should be sought.

In community property states, a spouse can bequeath only his or her one-half share of the community property, the other one-half belonging to the survivor.

This does not preclude one spouse from leaving his share of the community property to the survivor.

If bequests to charities or persons other than the wife and family are being considered, the wife should express her feelings which should be respected.

## WILL REQUIREMENTS

The formal requirements for a valid will vary from state to state. The maker or signer of a will is called the testator (male) or the testatrix (female). The provisions in a will may be informal but should be definite and specific. Two witnesses to the signing of a will by the maker are required in all states. However, some states require three witnesses. The designation of the maker and of the personal representative nominated by the maker to administer the estate may vary from state to state. The person nominated to be the personal representative is generally designated as the executor (male) or executrix (female).

The maker of a will can dispose of his property in any manner he choses and the provisions of the will must be carried out specifically by the personal representative. In addition to the usual provisions for distribution of specific portions of an estate, it is suggested that other provisions be included, such as the disposition of property in the event the wife does not survive distribution of the estate; in the event both husband and wife die in a common catastrophe. If there are minor children, provision should be made for a testamentary guardianship. If the will bequeaths sums or specific property to minor children, a testamentary trust should be set up for them. Minor children cannot own, possess, or control property in their own names. Hence it is necessary that a guardian or trustee be named to hold title for the children. State laws should be investigated. The testamentary trust should be discussed with an attorney or bank trust officer.

It is important that bequests of money should be made as a percentage of the total estate rather than of a specific amount for the reason that a bequest of a specific amount requires payment of that amount regardless of the size of the estate and the disposition of the balance of the estate. A percentage of the estate to be distributed is that amount computed after all specific bequests and expenses of administration have been determined. A bequest of a specific amount can result in a distribution of assets not contemplated by the maker and to the detriment of some heirs.

For example: 'A' leaves an estate of $100,000 with a specific bequest of $50,000 to 'B' and the balance of the estate to 'C'. Because of taxes and administration expenses amounting to $60,000 the distributable estate has been reduced to $40,000. The specific bequest of $50,000 to 'B' must be paid depleting the entire balance to $40,000. Thus resulting in 'C' receiving nothing.

# CHAPTER 7

# SELECTION OF A
# PERSONAL REPRESENTATIVE

Unless the maker of a will nominates a person, trust company, or bank, to act as his personal representative a probate court will make an appointment according to the priority appointment statutes of the state of the decedent's residence. Dependent upon state laws, which vary, the term "personal representative" usually means executor or executrix. It can also mean administrator. However, the term administrator is generally used in the probate of an intestate estate, which is one in which no will of the decedent is found. The will should also name an alternate personal representative.

After the will has been admitted to probate and upon appointment by the probate court, the personal representative is charged with the duty of preserving the estate by taking immediate possession of the assets of the estate and to prepare and file an inventory and appraisal of all the assets in the probate court. The personal representative is charged with the duty to collect money due to the decedent, to pay decedent's creditors, if necessary to operate decedent's business, to pay state inheritance and federal estate taxes, to sell assets if necessary to raise money to pay the estate taxes and administration costs, and then to distribute the assets of the estate in accordance with the provisions of the will. The personal representative is required by law to account to the probate court for all assets, income, disbursements and distribution of the estate.

Because probate prcedures vary from state to state we will not discuss probate and estate taxing procedures of each state. We suggest that neither a surviving spouse nor a personal representative attempt to probate an estate without the services of an attorney.

In most states the nominated personal representative has the absolute and final authority to select an attorney to probate the will and to represent the estate.

## NOMINATION OF A WIFE AS EXECUTRIX

Many husbands, for sentimental or other reason, will nominate their surviving spouse to act as executrix in the administration of the estate.

Irrespective of the value or the size of the estate, the simplicity or the complexity of it, unless both husband and wife have discussed and made note of all the items suggested on pages 8 to 27, the assumption of the duties and responsibilities of administration of an estate can result in a frustrating and difficult ordeal for the widow. If a husband nominates his wife to act as executrix, and he has not furnished her with the information we have suggested, he is placing upon her shoulders a tremen dous burden that, in most cases, she could have great difficulty in handling. She will be saddled with the duties of locating and marshalling assets, preparing an inventory and appraisal of those assets, the collection of debts due the estate and payment of taxes and adminis- tration expenses. She may have thrust upon her the responsibility of operating a business and of determin- ing which creditors have filed valid claims, whether to recognize and pay them. She may have to make deci sions concerning the sale of estate assets, and arranging for the transfer of property.

At the risk of being repetitious we must again em- phasize the importance of providing all the information hertofore suggested.

While the foregoing presents an awesome picture of the duties and responsibilities thrust upon a wife nominated to be the executrix, she does have an alternative. In many states the person nominated to be the personal representative is given the authority by law to nominate another person to act in his or her place and thus be relieved from the assumption of the respon- sibilities and duties of acting as the personal representative. It is suggested that husband and wife discuss the appointment of an alternate personal representative and to nominate such person in the will.

If, in the opinion of both husband and wife, the wife does not have a business background, is incapable of acting as the executrix, or is just disinterested, then some other person, trust company, or bank should be nominated to act as the personal representative. Obviously, whoever is nominated should be compatible with the wife. On the other hand, because of the husband's business experience and his handling the marital economic affairs, the wife, generally speaking, should nominate her husband in her will as her executor.

## PERSONAL REPRESENTATIVE FEES

Of great importance is the consideration of fees to be paid to the personal representative. In most states fees paid to the representative are established by law and are the same as the administrative fees paid to the attorney for the estate (See page 47). The payment of these fees has top priority. Consequently, if someone other than the wife acts as the personal representative, the amount of fees to be paid will actually come from the wife's share of the estate. If the value or size of the estate is substantial, the amount of the fee will be substantial. Since fees in most states are set by law, the amount of the fees can easily be approximated. If the estimate of the fee to be paid to another personal representative is such an amount as to deplete the wife's interest in the estate, then, regardless of her capabilities, serious thought should be given to her acceptance of the appointment as the executrix in order to avoid this cost of administration. The wife can always employ assistance at a lesser cost than would be paid to some other personal representative.

## ATTORNEY AND PERSONAL REPRESENTATIVE FEES

In most states, attorney and personal representative fees are established by law in a diminishing percentage in ratio to the value of the estate. As an illustration, the California Probate Code provides that the attorney's fees and personal representative fees shall be the same for administration services. These fees are set forth in the California Probate Code:

Estate of $1,000 or less:          7% of total estate
Estate of $1,000-$10,000:      4% of total estate + $30
Estate of $10,000-$50,000      3% of total estate + $130
Estate of $50,000-$150,000     2% of total estate + $630
Estate of $150,000-$500,000
                         1½% of total estate + $1,380
Estate over $500,000      1% of total estate + $3,880

This fee schedule does not necessarily apply to other states.

In most states, attorneys may not charge an arbitrary fee for their services in probate administration. However, in many states, additional fees other than the scheduled fees are permitted. These are called 'fees for extraordinary services' or a similar designation. These fees may be allowed only upon application, by the attorney, to the probate court for extraordinary services performed on behalf of the estate such as prosecution or defense of litigation, preparation of leases, sales of property, etc. The application for such fees must establish that the services were rendered for the benefit of the estate, that the actual services were rendered and the time required for such services. The amount of attorney and personal representative fees must be approved by a probate court order and thus will become a primary charge against the estate. While we have designated the court in which probate proceedings are instituted as 'probate courts' other designations are used in some states.

## FAMILY ALLOWANCE

Most states permit an application to be made on behalf of a widow and children for the payment of a family allowance. The payment of the family allowance is made from the assets of the estate and is usually a sum commensurate with the standard of living of the family. The court will normally make an order for payment for a limited time subject to a continuance upon an additional application. The payment of the family allowance becomes a primary obligation of the estate even to the diminishing of the assets of the estate and to the detriment of some of the creditors and devisees.

## WITNESSES TO A WILL

All states require that the signature of the maker of a

will be witnessed by at least two witnesses. Some states require three witnesses. The witnesses must observe the maker sign the will and then each must sign as a witness in the presence of the maker and the other witness.

In most states, before a will is admitted to probate, a witness to a will is required to testify to the mental competency of the maker at the time of the signing of the will.

In some states a bequest in a will to a witness is void. However, some state provide that under certain circumstances, such a witness could take the bequest to the extent as though there were no will at all.

We urge the maker of the will to be careful in selecting witnesses to the will and that no one named in the will to receive a bequest act as a witness.

## HOLOGRAPHIC WILL

While we have suggested that an attorney prepare the will, it is not imperative. Most states permit any competent person to write his or her own will without the services of an attorney. However, to be on the safe side, an attorney should be consulted with respect to special provisions that may be contained in such a will.

A will may be entirely written in the handwriting of, signed, and dated by the maker. No witnesses are required. Such a will is called a holographic will. No printing or typing may appear on the paper.

A holographic will should contain the usual provisions found in a witnessed will.

A holographic will may be changed by the preparation of a codicil. The codicil must be prepared in the same manner as the original holographic will and becomes a part of the holographic will.

The validity of a holographic will and a holographic codicil is determined by the laws of the state in which it or they were written.

In most states holographic wills and codicils are probated in the same manner as are witnessed wills and codicils.

## CHANGING A WILL

A will is not a contract nor an agreement between the maker and the persons named to receive bequests. The maker has the right at any time to destroy a will, to make a new will, or to make specific changes in an existing will.

Wills should be reviewed periodically and changed according to existing circumstances. This can be accomplished either by revoking the old will, making a new will or changing specific provisions in an existing will by the execution of a 'codicil'. A codicil is a separate document that must be signed by the maker and witnessed in the same manner as the original will. It must make specific changes in the existing will and refer to the exact page, paragraph, and words to be changed or omitted. When this has been done and the document witnessed, the completed codicil is considered to be a part of the original will and should be attached to the original will.

There are innumerable situations that could necessitate changing an existing will. Among them are:

1.  Are there any new members in the family?
2.  Have there been any adoptions?
3.  Have any of the beneficiaries died, married or been divorced?
4.  Have any of the devisees moved to another state?
5.  Has the named personal or alternate representative died or moved to another state?
6.  Has the named guardian or trustee died or moved to another state?
7.  Has the estate grown considerably?
8.  Has any of the property bequeathed been disposed of?
9.  Have inheritance tax laws been changed?
10. Should a life estate or trust be established for any of the beneficiaries?
11. Do you want to change any of the beneficiaries?
12. Have any of the minors attained majority?

These are but a few of the reasons for changing a will. Suffice it to say, a will may be changed soley upon the whim of the maker. Actually, no reason is required.

# CHAPTER 8

# CONSERVATORSHIP

Many states have enacted a probate proceeding to provide a modernized law similar to that of guardianship for persons in need of someone to look after their affairs without labeling such persons incompetent.

The proceeding is known, in most states, as a conservatorship but the designation may vary from state to state, as well as procedures.

In the conservatorship proceeding, the person appointed to take charge of the affairs of the conservatee is called a conservator. The conservator is given full authority to act for the conservatee, subject to court approval, and is responsible and accountable to the court.

The conservatorship proceeding may be used when either spouse is no longer physically or mentally, (because of advanced age, or other cause) unable to properly care for himself or his property. It is used for the protection of a person who is likely to be deceived or imposed upon by others. If the condition of your spouse is such that person or property is or may be in jeopardy, consideration should be given to the institution of a conservatorship proceeding and an attorney should be consulted.

## CHAPTER 9

# ADVANCE PLANNING FOR THE FUTURE...

Because death is a universal human experience, and because it has a profound emotional and social impact on the survivors, the customs and practices associated with it are very important.

Thoughtful people everywhere are turning to simplicity in funeral practices to emphasize the spiritual values of life and death, that simplicity can reduce both suffering and expense at the time of death and can more effectively meet the urgent social needs of the survivors.

It is never too early to consider and to make plans for the eventualities of death. Advanced planning is necessary to obtain both simplicity and economy. It is needed not only in making arrangements with funeral directors but the working out and understanding within the family. This can be developed by a frank discussion and planning at a time when death is not imminent.

When death occurs in a family in which there has been no planning, the survivors, under pressure of grief and shock, find themselves virtually helpless in the face of traumatic conditions.

The costs of funeral arrangements generally come as a shock to a surviving spouse and family. We therefore call attention to the existance of funeral and memorial societies that can be most helpful in facilitating funeral arrangements and pre-planning. Information can be obtained by addressing a letter to:

Continental Association of Funeral
and Memorial Societies
1828 L Street NW
Washington, D.C. 20036

# CHAPTER 10

# WHAT DO I DO NOW?

The shock of death is generally a severe emotional trauma. Most widows will experience the feeling of aloneness, loss, abandonment, pain and fear for her economic future, all of which will contribute to her inability to think clearly, to make decisions and her desperate need for comfort and sympathy.

Unless a couple has had the foresight to make arrangements for the eventuality of death, one of the first and most important decisions a widow must make upon the death of her husband is to arrange the funeral service, selection of a casket and cemetery plot. Many times a widow will be too distraught because of her physical and mental condition to make these arrangements and will need help. This responsibility will usually fall upon a son, a daughter, brother, other relative or a friend. Decisions must be made as to the time, place of the funeral and type of service.

In determining the type of funeral service to be conducted, the ethnic and religious backgroud of the decedent, and in many instances fraternal affiliations must be considered. Earlier in this book we suggested that the husband indicate his preference with regard to his funeral or the disposition of his body. If this has been done, his wishes should be respected. In some funeral services, religious and fraternal services are conducted jointly. If the decedent was a member of a particular religious denomination, the appropriate minister, priest or rabbi will usually be called upon to conduct the funeral services. The eulogy may be delivered by a close friend.

## FUNERAL COSTS

Dependent upon the economic level of the decendent and family the cost of funeral arrangements must be considered. There is no set schedule of funeral expenses. Funeral services, caskets and cemetery plots vary from place to place. The choice of the services, caskets and cemetery plots vary from the inexpensive to the costly. In some cases the desire for status by the family may be a deciding factor.

Occasionally, death will occur in some place other than the residence of the decedent. In such cases arrangements must be made for the transportation of the body to the place of interment. This, of course, entails additional costs dependent upon method of transportation used. If rail transportation is used, not only is there a freight charge but a coach ticket must also be purchased. A body can also be shipped by air freight.

## CEMETERY MARKER

It is customary after a certain period of time has elapsed, and dependent upon the religious custom and family preference, a marker is placed upon the grave of the decedent. In most cemeteries the upright tombstone is no longer used. A granite or metal marker with name and appropriate legend is imbedded on the grave at grass level. The cost of markers varies.

## DEATH CERTIFICATES

Death certificates are required to establish the death of the decedent. They are used to establish claims for life insurance, veteran's benefits, social security, retirement or pension plans, and to terminate joint tenancy. Usually the funeral director will order the number of certificates that he estimates will be required. If he does not, photo copies should be made. Death certificates can be obtained from the Bureau of Vital Statistics or other appropriate agency in the county where death has occurred.

## DISCOVERY OF IMPORTANT DOCUMENTS

Before a will is filed for probate, a thorough search must be made to ascertain if the decedent executed a later will and to find any papers or documents pertaining to the decedent's personal matters or to marital affairs. The following places should be examined: safe deposit box, briefcase, home and office desks, safes, lockers, trunks, suitcases, etc. It is suggested that all of the decedent's clothes' pockets be examined. Look for life insurance policies, accident and health insurance policies, disability policies, household insurance policies, business agreements, business books and records, bank books, saving and loan deposit books, promissory notes, deeds to real property, mortgages or trust deeds, pension, profit sharing or retirement contracts, federal and state income tax returns, W-2 forms and other records of earnings, social security number, marriage certificate, birth certificate, military discharge papers, Veteran's Administration claim number, motor vehicle registrations, installment book payments, receipt files, etc.

It is important that all documents and papers found in the decedent's personal effects be turned over to the attorney or to an accountant to determine if any have value, or if any have any bearing upon pending litigation or future litigation. Do not discard any policies of life insurance even though such policies may have lapsed because of nonpayment. They may contain some provision for death benefits and should be examined.

Upon learning of the death of a depositor, a bank will stop payment on all checks. If the account is a joint account of husband and wife, commonly known as a joint tenancy account, the widow should contact the bank at once and advise the bank of her husband's death and then take such steps as necessary to have the bank release the account to her.

## SAFE DEPOSIT BOXES

Upon learning of the death of a party who had access to a safe deposit box, the bank will refuse access to the safe deposit box until it has been released by a taxing authority. This presents a problem if it is known that the will is in the safe deposit box or if it cannot be found elsewhere.

Each state has its own regulations pertaining to gaining access to a safe deposit box. Depending upon state laws, special arrangements can be made to gain immediate access to the safe deposit box. If the key to the safe deposit box is unavailable, it will be necessary to have the box opened by drilling the lock for which a fee is charged.

If it is not necessary to gain immediate access to the safe deposit box to find a will, the box is usually opened after the will has been admitted to probate. Usually it is opened in the presence of a bank manager, the personal representative and the representative of a taxing authority or assessor's office.

## AUTOMOBILES

Claims to automobiles held in joint names must be made through the individual state Motor Vehicle

Department. You are advised to contact the state Motor Vehicle Department in your state to obtain information and forms. Automobile clubs usually handle details for members.

## PUBLIC ASSISTANCE AGENCIES

In many instances a widow will not know where to obtain information pertaining to her rights and benefits or where to file various forms and claims. To furnish such information there are numerous social agencies which provide assistance. Some of these organizations are the Red Cross, Salvation Army, Social Security Administration, Veteran's Administration and various church organizations. These agencies are more than willing to assist and when notified of a particular emergency many social organizations will secure the services of an appropriate agency.

# CHAPTER 11

# SOCIAL SECURITY

Of tremendous concern to widows is their economic future. Unless the estate left by the husband and the personal resources of the widow are sufficient to permit her and her family to continue the lifestyle to which she and they are accustomed, the problem of maintaining that standard becomes serious. If the estate is adequate, the widow and her family will not have to experience deprivation or any lowering of their standard of living. However, in most cases, when a husband dies, his estate is seldom large enough to produce sufficient income for his widow and children to continue in the previous standard they had lived. To help alleviate this problem the Social Security program of the United States provides financial assistance.

The Social Security system is extremely complex. Some of its benefits may be likened to an annuity plan for retirement years. Social Security benefits are paid to a family if the husband is totally disabled and cannot work. Upon a husband's death Social Security pays a monthly check to the widow and children or disabled children and in certain cases, dependent parents.

In the following pages we will discuss Social Security

only so far as it applies to widows and their children. It is not the purpose of this book to review all of the aspects of the Social Security system but to focus attention on the death benefit payments to a widow and her family. Social Security death payments are paid to the following:

1. Unmarried children under 18, (or 22 if full-time students).
2. Unmarried son or daughter 18 or over who was severely disabled before age 22 and who continues to be disabled.
3. Widow 60 years of age or older.

If the benefits are taken by the widow while she is between the ages of 60 and 65, she will recieve 71½% of the benefits to which her husband would have been entitled, had he lived. The amount payable to the widow at age 65 is 100% of the retirement benefit to which her husband would have been entitled, had he lived. At age 65, the widow is also entitled to Medicare protection which includes hospital and medical service payments. To be eligible for death payments, the widow must establish that she had been married to her husband at least 9 months before his death.

There are some restrictions to the payment of Social Security death benefits to the widow. She is not entitled to any Social Security benefits after her minor child or children reach the age of 18, until she reaches the age of 60. This is the best time for her to work. However, payments will be made if the child or children are attending school full time until they reach the age of 22. At age 60, the widow can receive reduced benefits or full benefits at age 65. If she becomes employed before reaching the age of 60 she will be building a Social Security credit fund which will determine the amount of Social Security to be paid directly to her. In some cases, the fund accumulated in the widow's account will entitle her to larger payments than she would receive if she took the payments from her husband's account.

Persons receiving Social Security payments are permitted to earn only $4,000.00 per year. If their earnings exceed that amount they will lose a portion of their Social Security benefits. This restriction does not apply to dividends, rental income, or other unearned income. This restriction on earnings only applies until a person reaches 72 years of age. If the widow remarries her benefits may cease but the payment benefits will continue to children up to 18 years of age or while they are in school full-time up to 22 years of age.

## FUNERAL EXPENSES

Many widows are not aware that one of the benefits of the Social Security Act is the payment of $225.00 for funeral expenses. Usually the funeral director will notify the nearest Social Security Office of the death of the decedent and will furnish pertinent information to that office. It is his best interest to do so because he is then assured of payment for his services.

# APPLICATION FOR DEATH BENEFITS

The Social Security system does not automatically pay death benefits. It is extremely important that the widow or someone on her behalf notify the nearest Social Security office of the death of her husband and request that an application for Social Security benefits be sent to her. Be sure to furnish the widow's address. The application for Social Security benefits must be completed with full information and sent to the nearest Social Security office. Should you not have all the information required in the application, make an appointment with an officer of the nearest Social Security office as soon as possible. The following information must be sent to or taken to the nearest Social Security office:

1. Certified copy of death certificate (proof of death).
2. The husband's social security number.
3. Your marriage certificate or proof of marriage.
4. Your social security number and the social security number of dependent child or children.
5. Your birth certificate and birth certificate of dependent child or children under the age of 22. If birth certificates are unavailable, provide other specific proof of age.
6. Employer's name and address.

You can find out the amount the government is

holding in your or your husband's social security account by writing a letter to Social Security Administration as follows:

Social Security Administration
PO Box 57
Baltimore, Md. 21203

Gentlemen:

Please advise me the amount credited to me (or my husband).

My name is _____

My social security number is _____

My husband's name is _____

My husband's social security number is _____

My address is _____

My husband's address is _____

I was born on (date) _____ at (place) _____

I trust you will furnish me with the above information as soon as possible.

Yours very truly,

_____

(Name) (Address) (Telephone)

## SUMMARY

To summarize, the amount of your monthly Social Security payment will depend on your age, when you start getting benefits, and the amount your deceased husband would have been entitled to or was receiving at the time of his death.

Widow's benefits range from 71½% at age 60 to 100% at 65. So, if you start getting benefits at age 65, you will get 100% of the amount your husband would have been receiving if he were still alive. If you are disabled, you can get widow's benefits as early as age 50, but the payment will be reduced.

Upon qualifying for Social Security benefits, you will start getting social security checks each month and they will continue to arrive each month until your circumstances change and cause payments to stop.

If you are employed and are under 72 your earnings may affect your social security benefits. You may earn as much as $4,000.00 a year without having any of your social security benefits withheld. If you annual earnings exceed $4,000.00, $1.00 in benefits will be withheld for each $2.00 in earnings above $4,000.00.

Since the Social Security Act was enacted by the U.S. Congress it is subject to changes. The foregoing rules were in effect at press time. We suggest that your nearest Social Security office be consulted for any changes.

## CHAPTER 12

# LIFE INSURANCE

The real purpose of life insurance is to replace the financial loss that occurs upon the death of a person. It is also an investment. We are primarily concerned with husband and wife and it is to them that we shall direct our attention with respect to life insurance. Husband and wife should discuss the purchase of life insurance. We are not advocates of any particular type of life insurance but suggest that it is a method of achieving an "instant estate" upon the death of the husband.

There are many types of life insurance policies to meet most individual needs. And there are numerous options of settlement of life insurance proceeds payable to the beneificiary. Life insurance has often been called an estate builder as it provides money immediately to the surviving spouse. As an investment, life insurance is a source of income. Cash value is always available for borrowing and can be converted at retirement into an annuity program. It is suggested that to avoid federal estate taxes on policies of life insurance on the husband, the wife be named in the policy as the owner of the life insurance policy. In this manner the proceeds of the life insurance policy will not be included in the husband's gross estate.

## SETTLEMENT OF OPTIONS OR METHOD OF PAYMENT OF INSURANCE PROCEEDS

In many instances a husband will have had the foresight to purchase life insurance with specific options for payment upon his death. The plan of payment chosen by the husband is irrevocable and the wife must accept the type he has selected.

The following are some of the plans available in life insurance policies:

1. Lump sum settlement. The widow is paid the entire face value of the policy at one time.

2. Interest option: This option is often included in the policy by the husband to protect his wife from dissipating the entire insurance proceeds. The funds are left on deposit with the insurance company at a guaranteed rate of interest. Interest only is paid to the widow periodically. The interest is considered ordinary income and income tax must be paid. If a husband specifies this type of option the policy should also provide that the widow has the right to withdraw part of the principle or to select other options. Otherwise the insurance fund would not be available for emergencies.

3. Fixed period option: The insurance proceeds are payable to the wife in equal installments over a specified number of years. The installments will constitute

principle and interest. Under this option the first $1,000.00 per year is tax free.

4. Fixed amount option: Another option provides that the life insurance proceeds be paid to the widow in installments of a specific amount until the entire fund is exhausted. The payments will include principle and interest while the fund is on deposit with the insurance company. Under this option the first $1,000.00 per year is tax free.

5. Life income option: With this type of option, periodic payments of an equal amount can be made to the widow for the balance of her life. The amount of the payments to be paid to her depends upon the amount of the insurance fund and the age of the widow. Under this option the first $1,000.00 per year is tax free.

If her husband has not elected to provide an option in the insurance policy and the policy is payable as a one-payment settlement, the widow has the right to elect an option suitable to her lifestyle.

If the widow wishes to take a single lump sum settlement and wants to leave the principal sum with the insurance company as an investment, or is not sure of what steps or arrangements she wishes to make, it is recommended that she take a partial settlement immediately, and later notify the insurance company of the option she has selected.

## PROOF OF CLAIM

Immediately upon the death of her husband, the widow or someone on her behalf, should notify the life insurance agent or life insurance company, whose name will appear on the policy, of the death of her husband. Life insurance policies name the beneficiary who should file the Proof of Claim. If the policy names the estate as the beneficiary, the Proof of Claim must be filed by the personal representative. If the policy names a child, relative or stranger as a beneficiary, the wife should seek legal advice immediately since her rights may have been invaded. In the event the beneficiary is a minor or incompetent, a guardian must be appointed. If a guardian has been appointed, the guardian must file the Proof of Claim.

Request for Proof of Claim forms should be made immediately to establish the death of the husband and to obtain the proceeds of the policy. The insurance company will usually require only two forms: Proof of Claim and death certificate or attending physician statement.

Before making payment, the insurance company has the right to demand information in addition to the Proof of claim and may ask that specific questions be answered. If this is done, be sure to furnish the information requested.

In the event it becomes necessary to notify the insurance company in writing, the following is an example of a letter to be prepared:


Salutation
Gentlemen:
My husband (full name) passed away on the _____
day of _____, 19_____. He carried (type of insurance policy) with your company, number (set out number) of the face amount of $_____

Please send me Proof of Claim forms and advise me what additional information or documents you will require.

Very truly yours,

_____
**(Name)  (Address)  (Telephone)**

### CHAPTER 13

# GOVERNMENTAL AND OTHER BENEFITS

Governmental benefits are paid to employees of the federal, state or municipal governments including service in the military.

The various divisions of governmental services for civilians provide numerous types of benefits, life insurance policies, health, accident and medical policies, pension and retirement plans. We do not intend to go into a complete description of all of these since they vary, but we will touch upon the important ones so that you, as a widow, will have some information that may guide you in making application for benefits, to which your deceased husband was entitled.

## FEDERAL EMPLOYMENT BENEFITS

1. If your husband was employed for 18 months or more by the federal government you, as his widow, are entitled to an annuity payment provided you were married to him at least two years before his death or are the mother of children by that marriage. The amount of payment is determined on the basis of the total years of service and highest average basic income received by your husband during any three consecutive years of

service. The payments to you cease upon your marriage before age 60 or death. If the benefits have been terminated because of your remarriage before age 60, the benefits may be restored if your remarriage is later terminated by divorce.

2. Even though your federally employed husband may not have worked eighteen months for the government, a lump sum payment may be available to you. This payment would equal the sum of the amount of your husband's contribution to a pension or retirement fund plus interest.

## PRIORITY OF LUMP SUM PAYMENTS

The order of priority for lump sum payments to the federal employee's survivors are:

1. His named beneficiary.
2. Wife.
3. Children and grandchildren.
4. Parents.
5. Executor or administrator of his estate.
6. Heirs as determined under the inheritance laws of the state in which the deceased died.

## GROUP INSURANCE PROGRAMS

The government maintains federal employees benefits programs. More than likely your deceased husband carried group life insurance and was enrolled in one of the group health plans. It would be well to investigate this possibility. In some instances a widow and children continue their enrollment in the plan and will receive benefits after the husband's death. If your husband had at least five years of federal service and was enrolled in one of the programs, the family coverage will continue as long as any one of the family members survives. As each member of the family become ineligible to receive the survivor annuity, the payments will automatically be reduced.

## APPLICATION FOR BENEFITS

Death claims are not paid to the survivors automatically. You, as the surviving widow, must file an application for benefits to which you and your family are entitled. the application should be obtained and filed as soon as possible. To secure an application form apply to the Civil Service Bureau of Retirement Insurance and Occupational Health (Civil Service Commission) 1900 Street NW, Washington, D.C. 20415. The completed application for benefits must be accompanied by a certified copy of the death certificate. The application for benefits may be filed at any federal office of Civil Service Bureau of Retirement Insurance and Occupational Health.

## STATE AND MUNICIPAL BENEFITS

If your deceased husband was employed in any capacity what-so-ever by a state or a municipality you must immediately notify the agency in which he was employed, or the appropriate personnel officer of the Civil Service Commission in your state or city. Ask in which insurance, pension, retirement programs your husband was enrolled, and his coverage, and to what benefits he was entitled. Benefits are not paid automatically. The state or municipal agencies will provide you with the information and forms with which to apply for benefits.

In many states and municipalities there are numerous benefits available to widows. Be certain which plan would be most beneficial to you and for your best interest.

## MILITARY VETERAN'S BENEFITS

The widow and children of a military veteran, whether in active service or not and whether his death arose from a service connected cause or death from a non-service connected cause may be entitled to financial aid for education under the War Orphans and Widows Educational Assistance Act.

The death benefits are divided into two categories: Death arising from a service-connected cause and death arising from a non-service connected cause. If the deceased died from a service connected-cause while on active duty or within 120 days after discharge for a service-connected cause, the government will pay the widow a sum equal to six times the veteran's monthly pay or not less than $800 nor more than $3,000. In addition, the government will contribute $250.00 for burial expenses and furnish:

1. An American flag to drape the casket.
2. Burial in a national cemetery.
3. Graveside interment and headstone regardless of where the deceased is buried.

After a funeral director has been contacted, he will usually advise the nearest Veteran's Administration Insurance Division of the husband's death and request that insurance claims be sent to the widow. In the event the Veteran's Administration has not been advised by the funeral director, you should immediately notify the nearest Veteran's Administration Center. They are located as follows:

In the Eastern United States:
Veteran's Administration
500 Wissahickon Avenue
Philadelphia, PA 19010

In the Western United States:
Veteran's Administration
Fort Snelling
St. Paul, Minnesota 55111

When filing the government insurance claim be sure to furnish the following information:

1. Decedent's complete name.

2.  His service or military service serial number.
3.  The branch and dates of his military service.
4.  Copy of his service discharge papers.
5.  If possible, send his government life insurance policy number.

If the above documents are unavailable, request the Veteran's Administration to assist you in securing the documents from the Department of Defense.

Before the insurance claim will be paid the following documents must also be on file with the Veteran's Administration or they must be provided by you. Ask the Veteran's Administration which of the following documents are on file so you can provide the balance. They are:

1.  Copy of death certificate.
2.  Copy of your marriage certificate.
3.  Copy of birth certificates of dependent children.
4.  If the veteran's death was service-connected the widow, the unmarried children under the age of 18, children 18 to 23 attending a veteran's administration approved school, disabled or helpless children and dependent parents may be eligible for dependency and indemnity compensation.

The following is an example of the type of letter you should write to Veteran's Administration:

Salutation

Gentlemen:

I am advised that you have been notified by
_____, funeral director, of the death
of my husband _____
who died on the _____ day of _____
19_____.

1. His government life insurance policy
number is _____.

2. His VA 'C' number is _____.

3. His military service serial number is ____.

4. He served in the _____
branch of the military (navy or coast guard),
from (date) to (date).

I should like to discuss my claim for benefits
with a Veteran's Administration representative
and should appreciate your scheduling an
appointment at (state date, month and time).
If you cannot schedule the appointment for
that date, please advise me of the available
times.

I have furnished you with all the information I have available. If you require
additional information please advise me when
you set the date for my appointment.

Very truly yours,

_____

(Name)  (Address)  (Telephone)

The amount of benefits are the same for wartime and peace-time service-connected deaths. The payments are determined on a schedule based on the pay-grade of the serviceman. Payments made to the wodow and children do not prevent a widow or dependent children from receiving death benefit payments from social security.

A non-service connected death may entitle a widow and her dependent children to pension payments. These pension payments are governed by the amount of death benefits income she is currently receiving and the number of her dependent children.

## FRINGE BENEFITS

There are some fringe benefits to which a widow and dependent children are entitled. There is an educational assistance program granted in certain circumstances and is generally paid for a period of 8 years.

Unmarried widows of members of the armed forces service may qualify for GI loans. Widows of veterans are entitled to a 10 point preference in applying for positions under federal civil service. If you believe you qualify for benefits contact the nearest Veteran's Administration Regional Office.

## ORGANIZATIONAL BENEFITS

Many unions, benevolent societies, service organizations, business firms, fraternal societies, automobile clubs, credit unions and others maintain plans and programs for funding death benefits for their members or employees. Many have life insurance plans, pension and retirement programs, and special funeral expense benefits for members. If, after examining all of your husband's policies, files, records, papers, etc. you find that he belonged to or was a member of various organizations, and you cannot determine whether he was covered by any insurance policies, insurance plans, or was entitled to any benefits you should write a letter to every organization in which your husband was a member requesting information.

## EXAMPLE OF LETTER TO ORGANIZATION

Salutation

Gentlemen:

You are advised that my husband (full name) _____ died on the _____ day of _____, 19_____. From his records and files I find that he was a member of your organization and believe that he may have been covered by a life insurance policy, belonged to a life insurance plan or program, or was entitled to certain death benefits from your organization. Would you be kind enough to check your records and advise me of any benefits to which he was entitled.

I should appreciate your checking and ask that if you find he is entitled to any benefits that you send me a claim form and list of whatever documents you will require from me as his beneficiary.

Yours Truly,

_____

(Name) (Address) (Telephone)

## PRIVATE EMPLOYERS

Many employers provide life insurance coverage plans, pension and retirement fund contributions, vacation, sick pay, terminal pay allowance and gratuity payments for their employees. If your husband was employed, we suggest that you personally contact or write his employer to ascertain if he was covered in a group life insurance program; if he was eligible for any death benefits or had due to him sick pay or terminal pay benefits.

In some instances a widow and children continue to be eligible for health benefits after the husband's death. To ascertain if your husband was covered in a group life insurance plan or was entitled to any death benefits, sick pay, vacation or terminal pay allowances, or if you continue to remain eligible for medical benefits, you should write the following type of letter to his employer:

Salutation

Dear Sir:

My husband (name)_____ died on the _____ day of _____, 19_____. He was in your employ until _____.

Will you please advise me if he was covered under any group life insurance plan or was entitled to any benefits such as pension funds, retirement funds, accured vacation, sick or terminal pay, gratuity payments, unpaid commissions, credit union balance or other benefits that I have not listed.

I should appreciate your sending me any claim forms which would be necessary for me to file and advise me what additional documents you will require.

Very truly yours,

_____
(Name) (Address) (Telephone)

# CHAPTER 14

## *Part Two*

# COMMUNICATION AND/OR NON-COMMUNICATION

In modern society the importance of communication is stressed more than ever. Many habits and patterns are formed in childhood which block one from speaking and sharing hurts, anxieties, frustrations and fears. Consequently, when these feelings have been bottled-up for any length of time one lacks the ability to express them (which means, ''I don't know how''). By the time of marriage, childhood patterns may have become so established that communication becomes almost impossible.

Lack of communication is 'what we assume the other person should know.' Because many couples 'take each other for granted,' and there is a lack of communication, they may grow apart. Learning to communicate with your spouse can become a fulfilling experience. This can be achieved by:

1.  First establish that you will not judge the others' beliefs, thoughts and feelings.
2.  Each will abstain from putting the other down and causing the other to withdraw, becoming defensive.

3. 'Listen.' Practice listening to what your spouse has to say. Each wants to be heard. Continue to talk together (not argue) until a basis for understanding has been reached.
4. Communication does not always mean agreement, but can include opposing viewpoints. Discussion should not be left unfinished but culminated on a positive note.
5. Whatever you expect from your spouse, give it first, be it understanding, respect or a listening-ear. Do not expect from another what you cannot or are not willing to give first.

These are suggested methods of becoming a mature, independent person through learning how to communicate.

## COMMUNICATION IS SHARING

Communication is far more than just conversing. It is sharing, questioning, and seeking to understand one another. Real communication is an openness and a sharing of innermost feelings. It is an open and frank exchange of ideas with each party giving full weight to the other. If your marriage has not been based upon real communication you may be experiencing a feeling of "being left out."

Is there real communication between you and your husband? Do you discuss the home, the children, finances, social life, friends? If these are your only topics of conversation, you are not communicating, only discussing or "talking about."

Many spouses question their marriage relationship. A wife will often ask herself, "Why doesn't my husband tell me what he feels," or "why doesn't he discuss his activities with me?" In truth, she should be asking him these questions. If the wife acts disinterested in her husband's activities, he may find others with whom to discuss and share. If the wife is indifferent and will not listen to his ideas, he may look elsewhere for a sympathetic ear.

Failure to communicate often gives rise to frustration and anger. By "leveling," being honest, and by an open and frank exchange of ideas and sharing of feelings, and especially their personal fears, the result will inevitably be a more positive relationship. If a wife continuously expresses fear of loss, such as her husband's job, she could undermine his confidence in himself.

Many marriages flounder because of the lack of communication. An important subject of communication concerns the effect of death upon the survivor. To be realistic, death is an inevitable fact of life. One must learn to accept the idea of death before it occurs. You may find it difficult to talk about death and what preparation will be made, but afterwards, it is too late.

Some may take an attitude that, "I will meet the problem of death when it occurs," without the realization that not being prepared or aware of the effect can lead to great unhappiness and a multitude of emotional problems. The following is illustrative of what could happen:

Although Betty and her husband were compatible, she refused to hear or talk about death and its possible effect upon her. At age 45, Betty's husband suddenly died of a heart attack. They had never shared their real feelings nor had they discussed the possible effects of death. Upon her husband's death she suddenly realized how unprepared she was to cope with her new status. Her friends revealed to her that her husband had often complained that she was indifferent, uninterested in his activities, and refused to discuss the subject of death. Their lack of communication left her with feelings of guilt and self-recrimination because of her attitude.

Should your husband become angry when you broach this subject, tell him there is no need for anger but that you are only sharing your thoughts and feelings with him. Should the subject of death be taboo and either or both spouses refuse to listen to anything that pertains to death and widowhood, there is no communication. Let him know that your feeling for him is one of love and warmth, but you both need to talk about and face reality. When the time comes that one of you does die, you will know how the other felt and how to cope emotionally. This understanding will make these emotional eventualities easier to handle and will alleviate many emotional traumas. To some, the effect of death creates a fear of the unknown which gives rise to many questions, some of which are:

1. What are my feelings about death? (This is a question that only you can answer.)
2. How does my husband feel about death? What are his thoughts and feelings regarding this aspect of life?
3. How do I feel about sharing my thoughts and feelings about death with my husband? (In spite of any reluctance on your part we feel that it is important that you share your thoughts and feelings regarding this subject with your husband.)
4. How would I handle such an emotional crisis should my husband pass away? (First, recognize your emotions, for what they are, understanding what you can do and how you can do it.)
5. Would there be a dramatic change in my living pattern should my husband die? (Yes, there will be many changes such as emotional, social and financial, and perhaps others.)

Your answers to these questions may be different depending upon your own emotional conditioning.

## TRUSTING

Communication means "trusting another." Trust is not always identified with love. Wives often complain that their husbands do not trust them. What does this mean? Trust is an emotion that expands with an intimate relationship. It grows with marriage and promotes harmony and understnding. Trust brings confidence. It is the basis for appreciation. Appreciation is the recognition of the role played in a marriage.

If you examine the possibility of widowhood with all the emotional changes that occur you could feel very uncomfortable and very unhappy. But would you not feel MORE uncomfortable and MORE unhappy if you did not know what to do and how to handle the same emotional experiences of widowhood, should it occur? Don't wait, think and reason now how important it is to discuss and share your feelings regarding this sensitive subject. Trust each other.

# CHAPTER 15

# MARRIAGE

## WHAT IS MARRIAGE?

Marriage is a relationship between man and woman. It is a legal contract; it is an intimate union. It is a relationship based upon love, trust, and companionship. To relate to a spouse, and experience a good marriage, the marriage must encompass understanding, sharing, and a wanting to do for the other and make the other happy, to be close, warm, loving, and giving with confidence and honesty.

A marriage is an emotional partnership which each must share equally. It is a joint venture in which both share in the "profit and loss" of their relationship. Sharing involves a responsibility as well as the enjoyment of giving and receiving, and each spouse must contribute to the other.

## THE IMPORTANCE OF AWARENESS

To be aware is an important factor in a good marriage. Every husband and wife should become sensitive to each other's strong and weak points. Until each recognizes and accepts the other's characteristics, communication will be difficult. Each spouse has something to give to the other. Each one looks to the other for that 'something' that they are missing within themselves, which could be strength, fulfillment, or a quality they do not possess. One partner can be more verbal and out-going while the other can be more withdrawn. One can be more intuitive, one less sensitive. One can be more social and the other possess more business acumen. In this manner they compliment the qualities the other does not have.

Every couple who live together have some antagonisms that are normal for two people who come from different backgrounds. There are many things in life that we do not like or want, but life cannot be experienced without them because no individual could possible satisfy all of our desires or needs. So we learn to appreciate the good and recognize the undesirable and live with both.

There is a common denominator that draws a man and woman together. It could be their background or similar positions, common interests in the arts, sports, music or nature; it could be similar behavior patterns, or a strong spiritual attraction. It could be just some basic need at the time they married. But whatever it is, it is more than just the physical.

If the wife wants her husband to be a success in his endeavors, she must encourage him to share his views and thoughts with her. She must show initiative and ask of him what he wants of her, what he wants of himself, in relation to their marriage. She cannot expect her husband to be honest with her unless she is first honest with him.

## MAKING A MARRIAGE WORK

The world has changed. Technology has now made it possible to breakfast in the United States and enjoy dinner in Europe. Many things have changed but marriage is still an institution and one that requires thought, consideration, and working out with the same fundamental effort as it did thousands of years ago. This is so even though established customs vary throughout the world.

The fundamentals of marriage have not changed, nor will they change in the future. There was a time when custom required the same ethnic background for marriage. Social mores have changed and marriages of different backgrounds are commonplace today, but the same emotional demands are made upon each spouse.

Because of the emotions involved in marriage, each union has its problems and trials, for no two individuals can be married without numerous adjustments, irritabilities, lovings and likings. It is not a static, but a working partnership and requires the effort of both. It takes the desire to understand, to share, and much patience to learn how to make a marriage work. It takes wanting, caring, giving, and affection.

# WHAT IS EXPECTED OF MARRIAGE

Marriage is a two-way street, even though some may find it difficult in the give and take, or in its reciprocal responsibilities. Subtle and general as it may seem, marriage alters people. Because we live in a changing world, we must allow for change in ourself and in our spouse. A happy marriage can result dependent upon the changes.

To be successful, marriage must have a goal. As an example:

Jack and Betty plan to retire at age 55 and spend their time pursuing happiness, travel, and enjoying each other. What will it take for them to carry out their plan?

1. They must agree on a common goal.
2. They must agree to share their ideas, thoughts, and feelings with each other.
3. They must be absolutely honest with one another.
4. They must cooperate, which involves saving money for traveling, and being heedful of their expenditures prior to their retirement.
5. They must have a working program, which involves keeping accurate financial records.
6. More importantly, they must have the desire to work together in almost every facet of their lives.

All things can be accomplished when two people are willing to give time, effort, discipline, to what they want to do with their lives. It is a joint effort. A marriage can be improved upon by the simple exercise of self-examination. This may be accomplished by answering the following questions:

1. Do I know what it means to be a wife?
2. Do I know what it means to be a husband?
3. Ask you husband what it is he does not understand about you. (Wife.)
4. Ask your wife what it is she does not understand about you. (Husband.)
5. What does my spouse want from me that I am not providing?
6. What is it that either of us may be doing that causes unhappiness in our relationship?
7. How can we gain a better understanding of each other?
8. How can we share more of ourselves with one another?
9. What can either of us do now that could make us more giving and considerate.
10. Are we entirely honest with one another?
11. What changes can either of us make to improve our marriage?

Many feelings of resentment and recrimination can be avoided with open and frank responses to the above questions.

The time for a wife to prepare, to learn and to become emotionally and mentally independent, is when she is happily married. The time to prepare is when you are in a healthy frame of mind for then much more can be dealt with, understood and resolved. When you and your husband are able to exercise reason, make logical decisions, you can then most effectively handle your affairs. When husband and wife are not under emotional stress, they will find it easy to have an open and realistic discussion concerning the aspects of life and death. The time to reason and prepare for any future eventuality is when they don't have to, and when there is no pressure.

## ATTITUDE

If you can remember that it is not what you say, and sometimes, not what you do, but it is your attitude toward what you say and what you do, that makes the difference. An attitude is a posture or position which shows the mental or emotional state of a person. Many attitudes are formed in childhood and become an integral part of one's mind and being. Without conscious awareness, these same childhood attitudes demonstrate themselves in adult years and especially in marriage relationships.

You can release the pressures of the past and let go of old negative ideas, though it will take new knowledge and more effort on your part. It can be worth your time and energy. Keeping emotions locked inside are injurious to mind and body. They are energy-molecules that must be released. Pent-up energy is explosive and suppressed emotions can lead to traumatic problems. While changing attitudes become imperative upon the death of a husband, it is far better to prepare yourself emotionally now than to undergo the necessity of required change.

The more a wife and husband talk about death and dying, instead of considering it as something taboo and to be avoided, the less ominous and threatening it will be.

Changing attitudes about death can bring a greater intimacy into the lives of married couples. It can bring moments of intense closeness and generate a greater understanding.

Two of the most basic elements of marriage are appreciation and consideration. Too many wives expect their husbands to take all the responsibility and do for them what they are not willing to do for themselves. In many instances a wife may not appreciate her husband until after she has lost him. Practice being thoughtful and considerate now and avoid self-recrimination later.

## CHAPTER 16

# THE PHENOMENON OF DEATH

## ABOUT DEATH AND DYING

For all appearances, when a man dies he no longer exists. Death is not an unusual exerience but an extremely earthy part of life. Perhaps the problem lies in the emotional feeling that when a person dies it is a permanent ending and that it is a total extinction of the person; it is the end and finish of life. While many believe this to be a fact, there are those who do not accept this idea.

Because of man's attachment to loved ones and friends, it is most difficult to accept their death. Emotionally it is devastating to lose someone who has meant a great deal. To a wife, the death of her husband may come as a complete shock and leave her in a state of emotional numbness. This particular emotion seems to be the experience of every widow and widower with whom we have discussed this subject. Some have said that they felt they were living in a bad dream and that none of what they were feeling, was real.

For many women, marriage is the nucleus of their lives. Upon the death of their husband they may feel their base is completely undermined. To protect herself from feeling the deep pain occasioned by death, a widow will sometime withdraw into herself. The first affects of death are numbness, followed by being oblivious to the passage of time. One widow described this feeling as 'spinning in a time-less space'. She felt she had lost her home-base. She went on to say that, "If I was confused when my husband died, it became even more acute later on when I realized that no arrangements or provisions had been made for me and that we had never discussed the effects of death".

The feeling that leaves the widow and widower most desolate, is the feeling of the void and emptiness that nothing at this moment, can fill. Many do not realize the emotional extent to which they are dependent upon their spouse.

Perhaps life is only a fallacy and delusion after all, yet one may want to delude themselves that they can live on and on. Because of the fear of loss or death, one suffers greatly, and the witnessing of death can be awful, terrible experience. However, there is a difference in the emotional reaction of a wife losing a husband as compared to the loss or death of a loved one or friend. The impression received as a child could leave its scars regarding death, with emotional drama played out and deep agony demonstrated by their elders. How often have we heard this expression, "Only a vengeful God would take a loved one away from his home and us".

Few people can handle their emotions when death occurs because of their strong fear of loss. It is necessary for one to change their attitude and concepts concerning death. While the aftermath of death is unknown, through understanding one's life, one can learn to accept the event of death. It is only by piercing the emotional veils of death can the strong emotion of fear be conquered.

It is not our purpose to propose that one become insensitive to the facts of life or death, but only to understand that this is a natural destiny which will eventually take place in everyone's life.

## WHAT IS DEATH?

Birth and death are each the most natural phenomena in the universe. We accept the idea of birth as a natural event but not so with death, because people fear the unknown. What is death? The eternal law of the universe is "that all who are born must die." Doctor Herward Carrington, Ph D., who has made a life-long study of death , spiritualism, after-death subjects, has written:

> "That no matter what view we may take of death, and, of what follows, we need not be alarmed, we need not regard it with horror or with fear. The power which brought us into this Universe and maintained us while here, whatever it might be, is quite capable of

maintaining a wise control in another life, if there be one. The 'present' constitutes the 'future' to those who lived before us while our 'future' will only be present to those who follow after us. In this or in any other world, life is probably continuous and progressive; and we have little to fear from the past or present so we have little to fear from the future. I should like to leave life at this age, just as one leaves a banquet, thanking the hostess and departing. Death is the last great adventure which we must all experience, though it is a tragedy for those left behind."

Death is a termination or the cessation of life. It is the transition from one emotional plane to a higher emotional plane. It is the separation of body and soul. Realistically, death is a process of life. The cycles of day and night cannot be changed for they are controlled by the rising and setting of the sun and moon, nor does the on-going process of life adjust to man, for he or she must change and adjust to it. Everyone must understand the inevitable, that someday some of his or her friends or relatives will die. Nothing is permanent, everything, every person must change, for, this is the nature of life.

Professor Shiro-Tashiro, of the University of Chicago, in his book, *A Chemical Test of Life,* wrote "...death is a necessary function in the process of evolution. Without death, evolution would be impossible. Death is not for the sake of annihilating life but that it might help and hasten the progress of life."

It is the intent of the authors to assist you in understanding the meaning of death. It is not necessary to view death with awe and fear. It has different meanings to different people and different cultures. To some it signifies 'suffering'; to others loss; to still others, desolate aloneness; and to others it is the end or finish of life. To some, it even symbolizes relief. Man has great fear of the unknown and death to man is unknown. To some, death is equated to the soul, it is a vague and abstract idea with little actually known about it. Death can also mean a 'rebirth' in the sense that an entirely new life can open up to the survivor. Few can answer questions that arise with respect to death, but the usual question is, "Why did this happen to me?" To many, the idea that the termination of life can be the beginning of a new one may not have entered their minds. There is really no need to treat death with awe and fear because it is an inevitable certainty of life.

When husband and wife can talk about death and all of its ramifications, before it happens, it takes the sting away from death. Not that it softens the blow of losing a loved one, but it can make it easier for you, the widow should it happen. It is written in the Bible, in Ecclesiastes:

> "That there is a time for every purpose and a purpose for every time; a time to be born and a time to die; a time for Thanksgiving and a time for sorrow."

## CHAPTER 17

# PREPARING YOURSELF EMOTIONALLY

What are emotions? Emotions are feelings. They are defined as strong, generalized feelings; receiving impressions; something that moves one deeply. Emotions cannot be seen intellectually, they can only be felt. From whence do they stem? The source of many of your emotions stem from what you absorbed from childhood conditioning and environment. They originate from your mind and being; from the subconscious and unconscious areas of your mind. Emotions are to be understood and looked upon as an integral part of you and, if negative, must be dealt with.

Every wife should ask herself, "What am I prepared to do emotionally, right now?" When a couple learns to talk things over and verbalize their feelings, they will appreciate sharing, which will lead to a greater understanding. Husband and wife should have no secrets from each other emotionally or materially. Perhaps it can be the recognition of unity, love, desire and emotion that neither had previously known. Emotionally, a unified front between two people can work wonders in a relationship. To understand each other's emotional feelings is the most vital requisite of marriage. You can learn to put your emotions to constructive use by keeping uppermost in your mind that what is important is that which is best for both partners. Emotions must be understood to have control of one's self.

Studying this book will enable you to have a more comprehensive understanding in dealing with your emotions. A good approach to emotional stability is to prepare yourself by conceding that widowhood could occur. Living is a risk which always encompasses a possibility of losing your spouse. By facing this risk before it is too late, you can gain emotional strength despite the forces of life and death.

Many husbands are reluctant to let their wives know that they fear death. It is natural and normal to have such fears as well as to want to overcome them. When you can talk to each other about your fears they will be more apt to dissipate and be less overwhelming. If your husband will not discuss the subject of death or anything related to dying, it is better to incur his **disapproval** or even face his anger, than to face what **might be** too late and too overwhelming, should your **husband** pass away. Refusing to face, to hear, to think and talk about death, or the possibility of death, is to refuse to face life. This creates a block. Look at the block before it becomes un-blockable. There are many things you can do to make yourself and your husband aware of what could happen.

1.  Do not wait until you lose your husband before making every effort to understand what might occur.

2. Learn now what you need to learn, before you are sorry.

3. You are not here forever, only for a short time, so use your time well to reason and understand yourself and your emotions.

4. To look at the worst that could happen, recognize it, see it and then face it, will make you less fearful.

5. To realistically commit yourself to living a full life is to look at it as it is and not the way you think it should be.

6. Appreciation of little things can bring contentment, it can also bring happiness.

When a husband and wife have discused the fact of death and its various aspects, they will then find it easier to understand and handle their emotions. Women are more inclined to be the implusive, impetuous and feeling partner of a relationship. Should the impact of death 'hit' and she finds herself a widow, it is then necessary for her to use her reasoning ability.

Widowhood can occur at any age. For peace of mind, it is better to prepare for the worst. Dale Carnegie, in his book, *How To Win Friends and Influence People* wrote, "When one looks at the worst that can happen, he is not afraid any longer of it happening." Should it happen, you can face it, because it will no longer be unknown to you. The question is, not what CAN happen, but what can YOU DO and how can you do it, when IT (should you become a widow) happens?

What you CAN do, before you may be left a widow, is to learn how to handle yourself.

## DISCIPLINE

The word "discipline" has been defined to mean training that develops self-control, character, orderliness, efficiency and, the ability to follow through.

An undisciplined mind experiences many conflicts. A disciplined person does not ask of another what they would not demand from themeselves. Discipline is vital. It is, in fact a quality needed to be practiced long before any eventuality occurs. Don't start anything and leave it unfinished, follow through on whatever you have deemed important in your life. When you make up your mind to do or refrain from doing something, do not let go of it until it is accomplished. A simple technque to achieve discipline is:

1. Discuss what is difficult for you.
2. Face what is fearful to you
3. Examine your true feelings.
4. Examine what reality means to you.

In this chapter you will become aware of what is necessary for your to learn, should you become a widow.

Ignorance is no longer bliss. You must learn what you need to know to protect yourself and your family.

Look at yourself as a person before your see yourself as a wife. Remember, you were a person long before you became a wife, or a mother.

Tell yourself that you no longer want to "play games" with your spouse and that it is important that both of you learn how to communicate with one another.

Know that you can be free of worry, hate, anxiety and suffering, and that freedom means untangling yourself from emotional pressures.

If you have taken the line of least resistance, consider the alternatives. While alternatives may appear to be less pleasant, disciplining yourself will pay off in the long run.

Discipline demands that you reason and work through your problems, analyze and examine the past and prepare for the future. It requires you to look at facts, alternatives, life styles and its changes, its ups and downs, its highs and lows. It is learning to make decisions that take much foresight and understanding. Discipline means decisions must be made despite the risk of making wrong ones. After all, any decision can be changed. .

# CHAPTER 18

# FOR HIM

It is statistically accurate that women outlive men. There are many reasons for this, probably because men exert most of their energies toward business. To many men the achieving of financial success is an important factor. To that end they expend more time and energy than to their families, wives and homes. It may be that greater peer-satisfaction is attained in business or a job, more so than in family life. Recognition is important to a man and consists in what he says, what he feels, and what he accomplishes. He wants his wife to acknowledge these attributes in him. Should she show disinterest, and they are unable to communicate about his business or personal activities, it could result in his frustration, annoyance, and eventually their drawing away from each other.

When a wife shows an interest in her husband's activities and is willing to be a sounding-board (even if she doesn't understand what he is talking about), whatever intensities he has accrued during the day, for whatever reason, her willingness to listen can dispel his tensions. Men, through their business experiences learn that nothing stays the same and that they must be alert and prepared for changes. Just as businesses are created and terminated, so does life terminate. Life ceases with death and it behooves every husband to engage in an open and frank discussion with his wife about the many aspects of death. When you are just as realistic about death as you are about your business, it will be easier to talk about the aspects of death and to face this sensitive subject.

## CHAPTER 19

# THE SUDDENNESS OF WIDOWHOOD

Undoubtedly you will have many negative, fearful feelings and many times you will not know what to do with them.

When a husband dies, a wife's sudden change from marriage to aloneness results in devastating emotional stress. The effect of widowhood brings on disturbances and feelings of being bombed out, almost as though one is in another space. When a wife finds herself alone she may feel she has lost her anchor and security, not knowing what to do with herself. Her first thoughts and feelings may swing from hurt to anger, to feelings of rejection, abandonment and hostility. One of the first questions she might ask is, "how could he leave me to face the resonsibilities I never had to face before?" Handling the sensitive and traumatic event of death, usually brings suffering and pain to a wife. Prior to her loss, she had her husband and now will she do, and with whom shall she share her life?

She may experience a feeling of hopelessness which creates a vacuum and the inability to think. Hopelessness is the feeling of futility, and a widow may feel, "What's the use, everything is gone and my world has collapsed, my life is over and I have no place to go, I simply cannot go on.''

Can you bring back your spouse? Obviously, not. While it is normal to feel dazed, upset, distraught at this time, the real problem arises when these negative feelings fill your mind and heart day after day, week after week, and year after year. Some wives are irreconcilable and refuse to accept the fact of their husband's death. In some instances they will not touch his room or remove any of his belongings, not realizing that this behavior could only result in mental and emotional disturbances.

You can spend the rest of your life being a continuing martyr to a fantasy. When you learn to reason and accept what has occurred, you can accept living from day to day. You may even be receptive to new ideas that may have been foreign to you, but which now may be exceedingly helpful. Ask yourself:

1. What can I do for others?

2. How can I make the rest of my life worthwhile?

3. What service can I render to God and to humanity?

By opening yourself to the spiritual qualities within you, you can learn to find peace in your mind.

# CHANGE

Humans are creatures of habit. Basically, we do not welcome change and widowhood brings changes. If living with your husband has been difficult and demanding, and he has been unreasonable and destructive, even to the extent of having abused you, you may resist change. The moment you are faced with change in your life style you resist and rebel. But if you did not experience change your life would become very drab.

One does not welcome change when forced into it. The first time a woman is compelled to make drastic changes in her life, such as earning her own livlihood, raising children alone, changing familiar environment, the probability of her resenting these changes is great. If in the past you were forced to make drastic changes, did you not learn to cope with them? Didn't these past experiences teach you greater understanding and an awareness of other areas of life?

Changes can be made as exemplified by a woman I counselled who I shall call Ann. After a marriage of eight years her husband suddenly died, leaving her with a six year old child. Her husband's death left her stunned, afraid and uncertain. As the days lengthened into weeks and months, she began to come out of her mental and emotional paralysis. She knew she had completely occupied her mind with living in the past and was failing in her responsibility to her child. Gradually, she took herself in hand. She realized she couldn't go on just sitting back waiting for life to bring her what she needed.

Ond day Ann looked at herself, as a stranger or an outsider and saw that she had gained weight, look older than her years and her attitude was that nothing mattered. Realizing that she had to help herself, she found a part-time job so she could be with her child part of the day. She went to night school two evenings a week, taking a brush-up course in typing and bookkeeping. After a semester she was ready for a full time job with good pay. She could now afford to enroll her child in a selective day care school. She started a program of reducing. All of this did not mean she had forgotten her husband or loved him less, for she missed him greatly.

Her thoughts turned to prayer, something about she had forgotten. Questions of God, faith and spirit entered her mind. She was now thinking, seeking, praying for answers to life. Two years passed and one day she met a fine man. He was the first in whom she became interested since her husband's death. A strong friendship grew between them and, in time, developed into love. Even now, she confided to a friend, that the love she had felt for her deceased husband still existed, but she was learning that love is not limited to one person and there are many different kinds of love. Ultimately, she and her friend married, and, again, change entered her life.

Some women may or may not react as Ann. Some

may bemoan their fate and live with the "ifs," which become a lonely and unsatisfactory way of life. The lesson to be learned from Ann is that there is hope when one puts forth constructive effort.

Prepare to make an adjustment or several, if necessary. A new chapter in your life has begun, and you must know that you will have to make changes as time goes on. Right now might be a good time to start experimenting in a new life style, a new way of filling your day-to-day time. It could be exciting, it might even turn out to be fun.

Acknowledge and recognize that a loss has taken place. Although you may find yourself frightened by it don't keep your feelings to yourself. It is important to your healing process to allow your feelings to show, don't deny them or cover them up. Deal with them. You are stronger than you think. You will survive. You are not unique. Many women have, with the loss of their husband, endured suffering and have become normal persons once again; so will you.

## CHAPTER 20

# WHAT DO I DO NOW?

"What do I do now?," is the cry of most women who find themselves alone. Because widowhood generally results in emotional changes, it is to a woman's advantage to prepare herself to look at life realistically so that she can handle these changes.

The suddness of widowhood thrusts a woman into different situations in her life. It is a different doorway that permits her to create new habits of thinking, new patterns of action, and learning to do things she might have feared. She can use her new situation as a sign to go ahead, handle the problems that arise each day and become aware of and appreciate her own hidden resources.

Even though you may have lost the one closest to you, life's values continue. The feeling of loss may weigh heavily upon you with despair and uncertainty. Until one experiences the death of a close one, they are unaware of the multiple emotions that could engulf them. They may suddenly become aware of experiencing feelings that have never affected them before. Some of these feelings may be:

1. The feeling of deprivation and hopelessness.

2. Doubt and perhaps the feelings of "this is it, there is no way to turn, this is the end."

3. A lack of a sense of reality as though nothing seems to have any real meaning at this point.

4. A distorted sense of values.

5. A feeling of aloneness.

6. Unconscious of the passing of time.

7. The desire to get rid of the deceased's possessions or to cling to them.

8. Indifference to the feelings of others.

9. Loss of the desire to dress.

10. A feeling of extreme sensitivity to hurt if not given attention.

11. Concentration on one's own misery and enjoying it.

12. Demanding approval or at the extreme not caring for approval.

13. Indifference to the feelings and opinions of others.

14. Dwelling on the past, fantasizing the best attributes of the deceased, and ignoring his bad qualities.

15. The facade of pretending to be gay or happy.

16. Irrelevant or disconnected acts because the mind is in shock.

17. Finding it difficult to sleep or eat.

18. Eating ot sleeping to excess.

19. The urge to talk a great deal or to remain completely silent.

20. Finding that material things have little or no meaning at all, including life itself.

21. Experiencing a sudden lack of confidence.

22. Withdrawing and hibernating and yet desiring to have people around.

23. The expectation of attention from others and feeling hurt if they do not shower sympathy upon you.

24. Making demands upon children and family.

25. Apathy toward work or finding solace in extra work.

26. The attempt to block out guilt feelings.

27. Impatience with others.

28. Indifference to a personal appearance.

29. Finding consolation in drinking or drugs.

30. Feelings of recrimination, of not having done enough for the deceased.

31. A feeling of relief at the death of the spouse.

32. Developing a stronger sex urge or losing it completely.

33. The sudden desire to do good work for others or engage in some kind of charitable work.

34. Loss of desire for creative or productive activity.

35. The desire to run away from home base, to different places for change of environment.

3. Deterioration of health and possibly elimination problems.

37. Becoming excessively extravagant

38. Becoming a religious zealot.

Emotions will be discussed in the Chapter 24, Page 141, "Handling Your Emotions."

What do you want most, now? Generally, the very first reaction of a widow is "I want my husband back." Realistically, this is impossible. So, now what? You must make some decision. The following are of prime importance:

1. See that you keep your body in good condition for health is of the utmost importance.

2. Learn to make your thoughts more positive,— to have peace in your mind.

3. Determine to overcome self-pity.

Because the widow's first reaction is shock, she can expect to be in this emotional state for awhile. The length of time depends upon the woman and how well she uses her mind. She needs faith as she goes through the tunnel of darkness and the uncertainties ahead.

This involves her acceptance of her new status, which is not easy and the realization that she must now make a life of her own. To accomplish these ends an understanding of herself is essential and neccessary for she has the power of choice.

She can either permit herself to remain in a state of emptiness or she can find a modicum of peace.

She can either become hysterical, which could result in a nervous breakdown or realize that her husband is gone and will never return. The husband she has lived with is no longer available and she must now come to terms by asking the question, "Where do I go from here?"

She must learn to reason and modify her reactions. One can reason to find solutions for immediate problems. Looking for alternatives for current adjustments in living is seeking for knowledge and growth.

These thoughts will help you to gain confidence and

increase the value of your own worth. Learning how to think and reason, make decisions and use your mind for constructive purposes will in many ways help to face this "changing world." Each person creates, his own happiness by appreciating the simple pleasures of life.

Your grief could be for yourself, rather than for the loss of your spouse, but that does not alleviate the pain you may be suffering. When a spouse dies there is a deep void and an emptiness. Every widow must accept a drastic change in her social status and look forward to making adjustments. Her immediate reaction might be one of feeling deserted and alone because she has lost her daily line of communication. She could even resent her spouse for leaving her and ending the pattern of living to which she had become accustomed. For the widow who is experiencing these feelings, it is not easy, for now she must rebuild her life. Spouses become habit-patterns to each other and one may find the loss of the habit-pattern harder to accept than the actual loss of the spouse. As long as feelings of grief persist they will block out any possibility of future happiness. Time is the greatest of healers and with the passage of time other people will fill the void and add new dememsions to your life.

Her attitude can be one of identification with lonely, unhappy and miserable women or with those who have accepted this experience as a part of living and initiated a new life for themselves. She can give love and receive love; give understanding and receive it. She can be the person others want to be with, and with whom others want to share. She can be interested in others instead of complaining, finding fault and expecting the world to feel sorry for her, making herself so unpleasant that her friends will avoid her.

Finding the balance in life is seeing every side of it; the pros and the cons; the good and the not so good; the highs and the lows. Being realistic about life and death is using common sense. Common sense means to think ahead, to reason, to look at the alternative, understand and become aware of what life really is. Life is a transient experience, for there is no one and no thing that exists permanently. Life is an ever-changing experience and we are like the chessmen on a chessboard. The positive aspect is, we have the power of choice to move these chessmen when and where we will, just as we can move our lives in the direction we choose.

Take each day as an opportunity to start a new life. Begin to evaluate yourself. What do you have? You have a mind, some knowledge, perhaps a profession, avocation, financial stability, children, a place to live, perhaps a car. What can you do? You can become a student, a waitress, an office worker, charitable worker, or something new that you have never done before. The solution or one of the solutions could be that if you feel despondent, use your mind and energy for something constructive. When there is a feeling that everything is lost, take stock of your assets, your attributes, and use your mind for anything good for your life.

## CHAPTER 21

# THE MOURNING PERIOD

The period of mourning should take whatever time you deem appropriate for your needs. Extending it too long will result in holding on to the past. Take this time to think, meditate, feel, cry and be alone. How should you act? Act as you feel and not as you think others expect you to act. Do not try to appease others during this time but ask yourself, again and again, how do I really feel? Do not be concerned about what kind of an image you are projecting, just be yourself. It's ok to be comforted. It's ok to need comfort. You may feel emotionally hurt, but time heals all wounds. Admit the pain, to feel pain after a loss is normal. It is proof that you are alive and a sign that you are able to respond to life's experiences. Accept understanding from friends, family and co-workers. An emotional wound is real, disabling and painful.

Some people are so good at comforting that they do it professionally. Feel free to seek help of a mental health professional with whom you feel comfortable.

Remaining distraught for a long period of time, however, is no proof that you really loved. In other words, don't feel duty bound to feel pain any longer than is necessary. Living is life-supporting and it demands that a person move toward joy and further happiness. You can and will survive the pain.

## PAMPER YOURSELF

People offer sympathy for physical injuries or illness, but not with emotional problems. You must understand the world simply does not cater to emotional pain. So pamper yourself. There are many ways you can do it; hot baths, massage, treat yourself to something new, get a manicure, take a trip, lie in the sun, read a good book, take time for yourself, see a good movie, etc.

During this emotional mourning period get more sleep and plenty of rest, which is essential to renew your spirits. Your mind and body need re-energizing. A meditation program provides comfort and calmness.

## CHAPTER 22

# WHAT TO DO AND HOW TO DO IT

Know that life goes on and that every ending has a new beginning. You are not a half-person but a whole person. If you want to isolate yourself and be alone then do not expect others to pull you out of your misery. You are only abandoning yourself, so don't look to others to bring happiness to you. It's up to you to set your wheels of action in motion.

The emotional foundation of a marriage determines a widow's reaction. Consequently each widow will react differently:

1. Some lose control and become hysterical.

2. Some assume a facade of grief but in truth are relieved of an unhappy marriage.

3. Some sensibly use their new status to determine what they can do to carry on their lives.

4. Some find a spiritual awakening with a faith in their own Higher Self, and they begin to search for their own identity.

## LIVING IN THE PAST

Living in the past is an emotionally dangerous state of mind for a widow. By keeping the past alive she is stagnating and ignoring the present. If she continues to keep her late husband uppermost in her mind, reiterating what he said, what he did, how he acted, she will be making comparisons with every male she meets. By constantly referring to her late husband, she will make others uncomfortable and they will no longer want her company. She will bore people with "what was" and not with "what is." In this manner she will close herself off physically, mentally and emotionally to any growth, change and happiness for herself. She could hold on to the memory of the deceased to the extent that she might actually be eliminating herself.

There is nothing wrong with living with some memories, but don't let them get too heavy. Enjoy them, but keep in mind, others are not interested in your memories.

If you find photographs and mementos helpful through the mourning period, use them. If you find mementos bind you to the past, get rid of them. Stop giving in to the past. Remember, life goes on. Making a new life of your own can replace many unhappy feelings.

A widow can learn to accept existing conditions (the here and now) or push unfulfilled feelings into the unconscious area of her mind. By living in the past, her present and future needs will never be fulfilled. She must get aboard the current train of life and let it take her where it will, for she cannot avoid finding new interests and excitement in her new experiences.

## CHILDREN

Children are emotional, too. Children need comforting. How does a mother tell her children their father has died and will no longer be with them? Obviously this is not an easy task for a mother, yet it must be done. In some cases a widow may be so involved with her own sense of loss that she does not consider the emotional impact this could have on her children. Especially at this time, children need as much comforting and consolation at their mother. It is a time when the family could be drawn closer together in their sorrow. Though this may be difficult it is a time when the mother, regardless of her own feelings, must handle her children in a sensitive manner. The children's reaction may not be the same as their mother's but the full impact of not having their father available may come at a later time. At this time the surviving parent becomes the head of the family and may take over the role of father as well as the mother's authority.

If you are filled with self-pity and give all your attention to yourself, what will you have left for your children?

You lost your husband, but keep in mind they have lost their father, also.

# POSITIVE GUIDE FOR A NEW LIFE

1. Determine to learn what is necessary for you to have peace in your mind.

2. Consider the situation and decide if it takes change to give you peace in your mind, then learn how to change.

3. Determine to recognize the necessity for change and set a goal.

4. Determine to use your emotional energy for constructive purposes.

5. Use the positive direction of your mind to "know what you want and, what you don't want."

6. Recognize your possibilities and potentials and allow them to come to the fore by taking a positive approach.

7. Keep yourself active and feel important to yourself in whatever you are doing. Determine to get interested in "service" activities or classes for your growth.

8. Obtain a job that will keep you interested and stimulated.

9. Let go of your adult children and know that they have the right to live their own lives.

10. If you see yourself beginning to wallow in self-

pity, remember that no one wants to be around a person who feels sorry for herself.

11. Take affirmative steps to make a new life for yourself by meeting new people, making new friends, attending classes and becoming a useful member of your community.

12. Consider a new career for yourself. All it takes is time, effort and determination.

13. Avoid living in the past by holding on to your late husband's clothes and mementos or anything that reminds you of him. If you are still married to him you will shut the door to any new relationship that could enter your life and that might be meaningful.

14. Learn to handle your finances.

15. Balance your eating and drinking habits.

16. Become involved with new, constructive hobbies.

17. Do not be afraid to relinquish the old patterns to which you had been conditioned.

18. Do not take on another's problems, you have enough to do in handling your own.

19. Worrying about tomorrow's activities could overwhelm you, so carry out your respnsibilities one day at a time.

20. If you find it difficult to uproot and eliminate

your negative emotions don't hesitate to seek professional help.

21. Give yourself positive attention instead of wallowing in pain and suffering.

22. Learn to pray. It will give you peace in your mind.

## CHAPTER 23

# THE YOUNG WIFE—
# THE OLDER WIFE

Death of a husband usually affects the older woman more than a younger one. When a young woman becomes a widow, with children to raise, she may feel resentful towards her husband for leaving her with this responsibility. However the younger widow usually has a greater opportunity for remariage.

A young widow with children is usually able to attract more companionship into her life. But with the older woman, what does she do? Where does she go for companionship? These questions can only be answered by each individual. While the older widow has less responsibility she also has less chance for remarriage because her opportunities for meeting new people are limited. However, in many instances she may not be interested in another relationship or prefers being alone. There have been instances where an older wife has felt hostility toward the husband for leaving her to fend for herself. In counseling I have had many widows, both young and old, ask this same question, "How could he do this to me?" They have also expressed resentment because they did not go first and that their husbands had made their future most difficult. Actually these are manifestations of their insecure feelings.

It is important to discuss one's feelings openly with one's spouse. It is suggested that all women, especially younger ones discuss the following questions listed below with their husbands to provide themselves with some answers if or when they should become a widow.

1. What am I afraid of?

2. Am I afraid of physical illness or suffering?

3. Am I afraid of death?

4. Am I afraid of losing my spouse?

5. Am I afraid of being alone?

6. Am I afraid that no one will be around to do things for me?

7. Am I afraid that I will have the responsibility of raising our children alone?

8. Am I afraid that I will have to replace the father image for my children and do things that I have never done before?

9. What would I do for my spouse today that I didn't do for or with him yesterday?

10. How would I act and feel if my spouse should die?

11. How can we be closer and have better communication today?

12.   What are my husbands feelings?

These suggested questions are not exclusive and additional communication in all areas will be helpful.

There are many reactions that a woman experiences at the death of her husband. The feelings of loss weighs heavily upon her, especially if she is an older woman. To what can she look forward? What happens to her social and economic status? What kind of social image can she project? She will be the fifth-wheel and will not be coupled any longer. Because of her new status the feelings of despair and uncertainty can set in.

Death, in any event, whether it be the spouse of a young or older woman, does not change the sad, unhappy and alone feeling of the widow. What each woman can do is to give thought to the possibility and 'take a look at what could happen.' Spend time together with your husband as much as you possibly can. Put your mental as well as your financial house in order.

## CHAPTER 24

# HANDLING YOUR EMOTIONS

There are many emotional factors involved in one's life. Emotions must be understood in order to be handled. They vary in intensity, moving from high to low key. Emotional shock is a prime cause of stress. Failure to understand our emotions can be detrimental to our well being.

The term emotions covers all feelings. In other words, feelings are emotions. Everyone is born with emotions which range from deep despair and despondency to heights of exhilaration and happiness. Emotions are both positive and negative. The positive is expressed in warmth, loving, sharing, giving, while the negative emotions are expressed in bitterness, sadness, resentment, hostility, etc. Emotions originate in the mind and heart, which are one. Both positive and negative emotions are demonstrated through one's reactions. A reaction is an opposing action, force or influence. It is like a rebound or a reflex within one's being. It is important to realize that when one gives too much attention to negative emotions, the reactions are detrimental to emotional and physical well-being.

You can learn to handle your emotions by becoming aware of your thoughts and attitudes. When you harbor hurt, anxiety, bitterness, you are allowing unhappy thoughts and feelings to consume you, you are nourishing the negative. Your emotions have taken over and you are no longer in control. Your uncontrolled thoughts and feelings have become greater and more powerful than your reason. Open your mind to learn what you can do for you, what makes you act and react to given circumstances; how you can handle your sensitivities to find some degree of happiness. Learn to think clearly and SEE what you are doing to and with your life.

There is an old adage, "Some people are committed to life and others are condemned to it." When you prepare yourself emotionally to face life you commit yourself to making it a place where you can grow, become knowlegeable, happy and productive. When you condemn yourself emotionally you are disapproving, critical and feel trapped. Instead of feeling free you inflict punishment upon yourself, expecting disappointments and failures.

Illustration: Mr. and Mrs. Kay had been married for many years and during the last seven years he had been seriously ill. He often said that he didn't want to live but also said he didn't want to die. During his illness Mrs. Kay complained bitterly at having to care for him. Sometime later Mr. Kay passed away. Did the expectation of his death take away the shock of his dying? No. She became hysterical and wanted to die with him. In fact, she said she would rather have him ailing and alive than have him die, for now she was really alone.

From the beginning of her husband's illness until after his death she ran the gamut of emotions.

An emotional reaction is a physical or psychological response to a situation or condition. To live in the past and hold on to yesterday's memories will make emotions stronger and more difficult to release. Depression and exhaustion of energies follows an emotional reaction. When you feel that everything is lost, allow yourself to experience the feeling of grief. Don't fight it. Give yourself time to take stock of where you are and what you can do to handle your emotions.

Many people say they want to get rid of unpleasant emotions. While unpleasant emotions can't be entirely eliminated, they can be changed by replacing them with other feelings.

## CHAPTER 25

# ANATOMY OF EMOTIONS

## SELF-PITY

Self-pity is a state of feeling sorry for one's self; it is a self-indulgence; it is a self-absorption. Sometimes one is not aware that his or her reactions could be predicated upon self-pity. If you indulge in self-pity you are wasting your energy and time. Self-pity can make you miserable, small and unimportant. Putting yourself in this position will only result in your feeling insignificant. It is as though you are telling the world, "I no longer matter because I am of such little consequence." Feeling sorry for one's self has never cured nor helped anyone. All that it has accomplished is for one to sink deeper and deeper into the quicksand of despair.

It is only natural for a widow to cry; it is a healthy release. It is not wrong to give vent to feelings, or to even be angry for the moment. This is more realistic than putting on a facade of passiveness and indifference. The person who feels sorry for herself feels that the world should revolve around her; that everything must be the way she wants it, when she wants it, and how she wants it. Indulging in self-pity will make others shy away from you. If you feel the need to commiserate with yourself, avoid doing so in the company of others, and allow this feeling only when you are alone. Remember, you are not a special case, but one of many millions who must find a place in this world without a husband. It is only natural for a widow to have periods of highs and lows during this time of her life.

Being extremely sensitive can destroy a widow especially when she feels she has become nothing without her husband. She can spend her time feeling sorry for herself because she feels she is not needed or wanted. If a widow feels she could attract more sympathetic attention, she might be unwilling to change her existing patterns.

If you want to feel important to yourself you must build a self-worth.

## ALONENESS

Upon the death of her husband a woman will suddenly find herself alone. With such a drastic change in her life she may become engulfed with fear and doubt.

Illustration: When Carlene was 48 years old her husband died leaving her financially comfortable. Although she wanted to remarry she thought it would be difficult to become accustomed to another man. She was open to a new relationship and in time she met a man in his early sixties for whom she felt an affinity. He told her he was fluent in several languages and travelled extensively throughout the world. He was interesting, exciting and she found him fascinating. She began imaging herself travelling with him. He told her he had not been employed for a year and was waiting for 'something to break.' He intimated he could use some financial aid from her and she assisted him. Having been successful in obtaining money from her, he then found excuses to terminate their relationship.

This illustrates how a widow who lonely and depressed is vulnerable to predators. It is not uncommon when a woman first becomes a widow that she is in danger of emotional involvement with a man who is looking for such a woman, who will be susceptible to his attentions for his own financial gain. The outcome of such an experience could leave a woman emotionally defeated and financially drained.

Companionship is beneficial but it is wise to be patient. With any new male relationship give yourself time before becoming emotionally involved, and learn more about his background, so you will not be sorry afterwards. Being a widow does not necessarily mean one has to be alone.

The following steps can help you to replace aloneness:

1. Make a decision about what you want and how you will obtain it.

2. Determine that this is a time to learn, to move out into the world. Replace depression and

lonely feelings with constructive activity.

3. Start doing for others who need your help. There are many charitable institutions that can use volunteers.

4. Open your mind by attending classes and lectures.

5. Remember that there are many men and women out there who need and want your smile, your warmth, your encouragement the same as you want theirs.

6. Find someone with whom you can share mutual interests.

Some people are loners all their lives and may be able to handle aloneness. For those who find it difficult, it is suggested that you answer these questions. What did you do before marriage? Were you engaged in any vocation? Were you occupied with interesting activities, family or friendships? To replace aloneness pursue those same directions. You must determine that if you are going to make a new life for yourself start the rebuilding process as soon as you feel able.

Solitude can be comforting, but not to the exclusion of family and friends.

# DEPRESSION

The woman who feels 'down' may prefer to remain within her own boundaries which could be her home, her bedroom, her couch or her children. With her spirit sinking lower and lower she clings to that which is familiar and comfortable. This could happen to the depressed widow who feels pained and hurt, grieving for what she had.

When a widow is depressed nothing seems to have any value and all appears to be distorted. There is a complete absence of stimulation or excitement and she could feel that she is unwanted, unneeded, unloved and a burden to others.

Sometimes after the death of a husband, a widow could feel that she has lost her identity. The realization of this loss, of what she had been, or her status as a wife, could prove to be a depressing experience.

Illustration: Two years had passed since Edith's husband died leaving her with two teen-age girls to whom she is devoted. She has no social life although she had the opportunity to meet many people in her job. she is continually in a state of despair and depression. This presents two questions; is she depressed because her husband died or is she feeling sorry for herself? These questions are important because each widow must answer them for herself.

As long as one dwells on the negative nothing will change. Depression is a state of mind which can be changed and everyone has the power to replace his or her thoughts, look for something of a positive nature and dwell on it. It takes less energy to look for and dwell on something positive than it does to hold on to the negatives.

## GUILT

Guilt is a powerful feeling of self-reproach resulting from a belief that one has done something wrong or immoral. The first guilt comes from neurotic suffering as a child. It is self-imposed and we usually learn the meaning of this feeling from childhood when we were told that "if you do not behave you be punished." You might have even heard it said that "one day you might suffer as you have made your parents suffer."

A widow's feelings of guilt could arise when she believes that she should have done or could have done or ought to have done more for her husband when he was alive. If the widow persists in holding on to these feelings she will be furthering her guilt. She will continue to punish herself, becoming bitter and resentful, making herself and those around her unhappy. Guilt is often used in self-recrimination and repeated admissions of guilt tend to create an unwarranted justification of actions. One could feel guilty for berating and putting down a spouse unjustifiably. Guilt is often used as an excuse for one indulging in self-pity.

Illustration: Bette's husband passed away suddenly and for two years she often spoke of the feelings of guilt she had because of what she could have done differently when Carl was still alive. Because of her strong feelings she decided to seek counseling. It was then that she admitted she was angry with Carl because he had not left a will nor organized their affairs so that she could adequately handle the estate. She had been unaware of her anger, but was aware only of her guilt. She had never really taken any interest in what Carl was doing but took for granted that he would always be there to take care of her financially. When Bette became a widow her guilt feelings made her ill. She realized that she had not encouraged any real communication with Carl, since she was too busy socializing. Now she is punishing herself. This is an example of how guilt can affect one physically.

Guilt can be overcome by:

1.  Analyzing its cause or reason (Why do I feel guilty?)

2.  Recognize and accept the cause.

3.  While it is impossible to change the cause of guilt, the feeling can be mitigated by the realization and understanding of the original cause.

You may think that how you act or react goes un-
noticed by others but you cannot cover up your feelings.
Many times there is a deep resentment between
husbands and wives and this resentment intensifies
because of the non-communication of feeling that each
keeps to him or herself. It is only when feelings are
openly discussed that the air is cleared and the way
opened for better understanding between two people.

## HURT/RESENTMENT/BITTERNESS

Webster defines resentment as a feeling of bitter hurt
or indignation; it comes from a sense of being injured or
offended. The feeling of resentment often arises when a
husband dies and the wife feels indignant because in her
mind, he should not have left her alone and unprepared
for a completely different way of life. These thoughts
could build up feelings of bitterness. Should she continue harboring these feelings of hurt and resentment
towards her husband, she will become a neurotic, bitter
person. Her resentful thoughts will affect no one but
herself. Because of her guilt feelings, oftentimes a wife
will feel that her husband's death was a punishment
directed at her. The feelings could stem from the belief
that she failed to give her spouse more attention and
consideration.

Many times sudden aloneness generates bitterness.
Then consider, did you not have a husband and companion for many more years than some women? Did
you have someone who loved you? If so, then you are

more fortunate than many who knew only happiness in a brief marriage but who appreciated their being loved, if only for a short time. For us to make the statement that there should be no bitterness would be presumptive because it is a natural reaction. Understanding your emotions can help you to overcome any such feelings.

One of the women we interviewed had been a widow for several years and told us of her appreciation for her husband and that she was grateful for the twenty-five years she had lived with her 'wonderful friend and companion,' and that she had had more than many women who did not know such warmth and love from a man. She is now busily engaged planning a memorial of his works since he was a musical composer-director. She is assembling all of his memorabilia. She feels that if she had gone first he would not have published his music and so she is busily occupied in this project that she has made for herself. She considers the fact that he died first an advantage, in that she would never have known that she could accomplish this tremendous feat. She is mingling with people, sharing and giving of herself and finding value in life.

Her option could have been hurt, bitterness, resentment, anger, self-pity, expecting sympathy from her children and friends, but she does not expect anything from anyone. She accepted her change of status and made new friends. She has come to terms with what is this day in her life. Her new concept has made her a happier and more acceptable person to herself and to others. She feels re-born and this is her reward. She has taken advantage of her changed status to find herself.

## REJECTION

Rejection means a casting off, a foresaking of, a repudiation.

A wife may feel that when her husband dies she has been rejected. Examples of rejection could encompass many of the following areas: the widow no longer has her companion. She is on her own, with many women with whom she must compete. With her husband she was safe and protected and had someone upon wom to lean. Now, she is just another single woman who is not accustomed nor conditioned to face people, places and things alone. Having relied upon her husband for support and companionship her world is shattered and now she feels rejected.

She may have been the clinging-vine type who encouraged her husband to take care of her, support her emotionally, mentally, and physically; she may have been the perpetual child who looked to her 'daddy' (husband) to care for her. She may have been the hypochondriac who was always sick but could always depend upon her husband for sympathy and attention,and she may have been the helpless one who could not make a decision or think for herself and waited for his word, his decision, his direction. Now she has no one, for in her mind no one will ever again cater to her like he did, and this she interpretes as rejection.

Recognize that no one can live in this world without having been rejected at some time or rejecting another.


# FEARS

Fear is the feeling of painful apprehension, uncertainty, doubtfulness, and fright of the unknown.

Throughout the ages man has feared the unknown, of which death has been paramount. The fear of living and being unable to cope with life can be as strong as the fear of death. It is best that fear be examined before the death of a spouse and before it is too late.

When fears grow and become stronger than you, they can eventually rule you. Fear is an overwhelming energy that builds and expands the more it is dwelt upon. It absorbs your every thought, idea and feeling, until you become one big fear and lose your perspective. Unless you discipline, control and redirect your fears, they will run rampant. Many give fears so much power that they must manifest and project into their lives. When the emotional cause of fear is understood it can be replaced with positive thoughts. When the unknown becomes known, there is nothing left to fear.

## FEAR OF LOSS

The greatest fear of all is a sense of loss and the most difficult to bear and accept. With a sense of loss comes depression and great insecurity.

In this context the word "loss" is used to mean the fear of being deprived of a loved one by death. Because of this fear of loss there is a reluctance to face or discuss the uncomfortableness of what might or could happen.

Living in fear is suffering, but facing it will cause it to dissipate. The fear of not having is the fear of loss. Fears can destroy you because they stem from within. You can learn to uproot them by replacing them with positive attitudes. The fear of losing may prevent you from appreciating that which you already have.

Deep negative emotions can bring on strong fears which can block your mind from reasoning and thinking clearly. Consider the following questions:

Are you afraid of losing material possessions? of hurting others or being hurt? of communicating with those close to you? of rejection? of the opinions of others? of love? of your spouse? of being alone and being abandoned? of helplessness? or responsibility, such as raising a family? of having to earn your own living? of illness? of dying? of guilt feelings?

By answering these questions, which must be based on your own personal feelings, you will be able to examine your fear and have a better understanding of yourself.

## FANTASY AND REALITY

Widowhood does happen and can happen at any age. It is best that you prepare for this eventuality now. We are not suggesting that you look forward to widowhood, but that you face this probability and cease living in a fantasy world "that this could never happen to me."

Fantasy has been defined as make-believe; a day dream; an illusion; a dream world; wishing and hoping to live in a way that one would constantly like; like living in a Shangri-la; a figment of your imagination. A fantasy is seldom based on positive thoughts. Fantasy is an indulgence, a substitute for reality. It is used at times to cover up what we don't want to see or acknowledge. Fantasy is often used as a refuge to justify one's actions. Fantasy often results in a sense of false security, because at the end of the fantasy there is reality. The following are some of the commonplace fantasies:

They are used to cover up the real world which is threatening to you and which you do not wish to face. They are often used to counteract 'put-downs,' to reinforce ego and to disbelieve the truth; either spouse can blame the other for lack of understanding; either can say, "I didn't hear you," when you really don't want to listen; either spouse can take refuge in sleep when words are too painful. Believing the subject would be too hurtful and painful to the other, you or your husband may avoid a discussion of death and dying. Either of you may prefer to live in the fantasy, that nothing will ever change, but that things will always be just at they are. In reality your concern is not discussing a subject that is painful to your spouse, but actually is painful to you.

Some take refuge in a make-believe world such as not wanting to grow up, and always imagining themselves as a child who has no responsibility. Some imagine themselves to be something they are not and play games with reality. A commonplace fantasy is the romanticising of a deceased spouse, when in truth and fact he was most difficult to live with.

## EMOTIONAL RESPONSE TO REALITY

Reality is that which exists here and now. Reality is what IS today. Reality is understanding that negative attitudes bring suffering, while positive atitudes bring growth and change. It is recognizing the importance of making decisions so that one can function as a whole person.

If one is experiencing emotional pain it must be acknowledged, examined and then faced. Reality may be painful to face but what is the alternative? Some women withdraw from reality and neglect themselves. A widow, fantasizing that she will find peace and serenity if she joins her deceased husband, is not living in reality, for life still beckons her. Widows must recognize existing conditions as they are. Her social status is changed, and she is a single rather than a "we." Nothing in the future will ever be the same; today is the only NOW that counts. This is the reality every widow must accept.

Fantasies remain fantasies. For the most part they seldom go anywhere. On the other hand reality can result in productivity and awareness. Pain and discomfort brought on by problems, cannot be wished away. Time, energy, perseverance and the will to overcome negativity will help you to replace them with positive attitudes.

You can change a fantasy into a reality by using it as a constructive tool for a specific purpose and by imagining yourself strong, firm and capable, handling your emotions until belief becomes a reality.

## ANGER

Anger can be a smoldering rage within you or be manifested in overt actions of wrath and ire. It is a form of resentment. Anger is insidious in that it can build in intensity. Because of a husband's death a widow could harbor inner anger and resentment. She could feel lost and deserted. Because of these feelings she could realize that she had been sheltered in a cocoon of comfort and protection and was now angry that she would have to fend for herself.

It's ok to feel anger. Everyone gets angry occasionally. Let your anger out by hitting a pillow, yell, scream, or cry. Crying, for a widow, is the best form of release. Cry out your sadness and hurt. Anger can be a natural reaction to a husband's death. When your anger is dissipated in these harmless ways you will avoid anxiety, depression and physical discomfort. Anger will vanish as grief subsides.

It is necessary to learn to change your thoughts and feelings to achieve contentment and peace in your mind which means, "I know now how to handle me."

## CHAPTER 26

# THE MIRACLE OF YOUR UNFAILING MIND

All through part Two we have stressed pertinent points relating to the handling of marriage and emotions. Perhaps few couples recognize to what degree the mind is responsibile for the emotions in a marriage relationship. We have made you aware of many important aspects of living, but it takes the Miracle of Your Unfailing Mind to bring them into focus.

To be able to handle and resolve problems, you must have an understanding of your emotions. To accomplish this, your mind must function clearly. By learning to come to terms with yourself, you will bring some harmony into your life.

One of the most feared and misunderstood facts of life is the acceptance of death. The naturalness of this phenomenon is a miracle. When you recognize and understand, you will soon realize it is an experience which will eventually occur to everyone.

Your unfailing mind is your "tool" to help you comprehend this natural phenomenon with the least amount of pain and suffering. It is a miracle that we live and die, as all living things complete the same cycle.

Your mind will never fail you when you once learn to discipline it and use it for constructive purposes. The miracle is that everyone is born with this tremendous mechanism. You have been endowed with the power to change, to feel, to direct your thoughts and attitudes. By using your mind you will learn to understand, accept and replace one thought with another and one idea with another. You will be able to replace negative feelings with positive ones. Only through the Miracle of Your Unfailing Mind will you be able to 'let go' and relinquish deep negative hurts.

There has to be a dependency upon something, other than a husband, that will not fail a wife. The one thing she can depend upon is the Miracle of her Unfailing Mind. When a husband and wife can read and study, follow and adhere to the ideas, questions and directions set out in this book, they will then discover how imperative it is to reason, to make decisions and to use the Power of Your Unfailing Mind to communicate and put your business and domestic affairs in order.

YOU HAVE THIS MIRACLE. USE IT WISELY. IT IS YOURS ALONE, AND NO ONE CAN TAKE IT FROM YOU. *TRUST IT. DIRECT IT.*